CHRISTIAN FAITH SERIES
Reinhold Niebuhr, CONSULTING EDITOR

THE STRANGENESS OF THE CHURCH

BOOKS BY THE SAME AUTHOR

Congregationalism: A Restatement

Prayer and the Service of God

Gift of Ministry

Church Meeting and Democracy

Nature of Catholicity

Britain and the Future

The Strangeness
of the Church

BY DANIEL JENKINS

Doubleday & Company, Inc., 1955
Garden City, New York

Library of Congress Catalog Card Number 55-8404

2 61
J 5 2

Contents

11157

THE STRANGENESS OF THE CHURCH

CHAPTER I

The Strangeness of the Church

What is strange about the Church? A church in another country or of an unusual denomination may seem strange, but to most people in Western lands the Church as they know it is one of the most ordinary and obvious of institutions. Even if they rarely attend it, or are doubtful about the validity of the faith it professes, the old church on the green or the little church around the corner is likely to be as familiar and its activities as calculable as any of the other institutions closely associated with their childhood.

This superficial familiarity may, however, be one of the greatest barriers to understanding the true nature of the Church. It requires a considerable effort of thought and imagination to see the Church in the right setting, especially for those who think of it only in terms of the settled and prosperous churches of America and Western Europe. The various churches of these lands are so closely bound up with the life and attitude of the prosperous and respectable sections of the community that it is hard to make a clear distinction between them and society in general. It becomes natural to think of

them either as voluntary societies of varying degrees of dignity
and influence or else as the institutional expression of one aspect of the life of their nation. But this is to be misled. The
Church cannot be understood or evaluated only in terms of the
showing made within living memory by the institutions bearing that name. It must be considered in the light of the whole
history of those who have called themselves the people of God,
from Abraham's time to Christ's, and from Christ's time to our
own day.

When the Church is looked at from this point of view, its
strangeness becomes much more manifest. For in the perspective of history, the Church stands out as the most remarkable
institution or group of institutions the world has ever seen. If,
in the most general and inclusive way, we define the Church as
the whole company of those who have publicly confessed their
allegiance to the God who has revealed Himself in Christ, we
can say that it has persisted as a strong and effective focus of
men's loyalty longer than any nation which is prominent in the
modern world. Some other religious movements, notably in the
East, can make a similar claim, but they have not shown a like
ability to maintain themselves amid sweeping changes and to
take root among people of the most diverse race, language,
nation, and level of culture. Buddhism has spread through
many countries of the East, but it seems unable to find much
point of contact with the Western world. Islam has an intense
grip upon its followers, but it does not show much ability to
extend very far beyond the lands of the tropical desert. Judaism alone is comparable to the Church in this respect, and
Judaism has a relation to the Church which is peculiar and
intimate. In this age, the connection between the Church
and the Western world is most obviously before men's eyes, but
it was founded in a land which was more Eastern than Western,
and it still retains a tenacious influence in some parts of the

East, despite its difficulties in China. It is extending its influence in other parts, notably in India and Southeast Asia.

The quality of the Church's influence is no less remarkable than its extent. A strong case can be made for the claim that in the West the Church has been the greatest single influence in the development of the world. It is widely recognized that it was the dominant influence in the Middle Ages, but it has been hardly less powerful in the formation of the modern world as well. The Church has been the source and inspiration of an immense part of our cultural heritage. This is especially true in relation to music and architecture, but only quite recently Miss Rose Macaulay had occasion to observe that more good books in English had been produced by clergymen on more subjects than by any other group in the community. The Church's educational influence has been immeasurable. Its positive effect even on the development of the modern science which has often looked at it with grave suspicion has been greater than it is fashionable to acknowledge, as Whitehead used constantly to remind us. Its influence on political ideas and institutions has been very substantial, even though it may often have been indirect.

It is worth remembering all this when the triviality and weakness of some modern churches fills the picture, but our opening question still remains. It may prove that the Church may have a claim to be regarded as outstanding among human institutions, but that does not make it strange. The strangeness of the Church lies, rather, in that while it stands in the midst of the everyday life of the world, it yet makes unusual claims for itself and displays unusual qualities in justification of them. It is a society of men of like nature with their fellows which claims to be founded by God. It asserts that this God is the creator and sustainer of all things, the final reality with whom all men have to deal, and that He has revealed Himself in a

series of historical events which have reached their decisive
culmination in Jesus Christ, who stands in a special relation to
Him. The Church claims that it has come into being through
the action of this God in Jesus Christ and that this God continues to guide and rule it in His Spirit. It also claims that it
provides the chief means by which His purpose for mankind
can be discovered and fulfilled.

In the face of this it might be retorted that, on the contrary,
the strange thing about the Church is not this claim but its
spectacular failure to make it good. Churches profess to offer,
in the name of this God, an effective message of reconciliation
and universal brotherhood, yet they reflect the divisions of the
world about them and have often persecuted each other. They
profess to teach men the humility of Christ and the need for
service, yet they have constantly been used as vehicles of personal ambition and as battlegrounds between rival power
groups. They profess to bring the means of refreshment and
renewal to men, yet they have degenerated into a pettiness
and a triviality worse than those of the world about them. Is
the abundant life of which the churches so freely speak simply
a matter of ladies' sewing meetings and tame fellowship eve-
nings for unadventurous young people? These well-known
facts have led many people, particularly in the modern world,
to repudiate the Church even when they acknowledge some
validity in the teaching of Christ. They contrast Christianity
with Churchianity and speak with dramatic fervor of the betrayal of Christ by the churches.

That men should be so perverse is indeed, from one point of
view, the strangest thing in life, but it is doubtful whether that
in itself constitutes the heart of the strangeness of the Church.
For the failure of men to live up to their ideals is one of the
most familiar facts of experience. It is the way in which we are
accustomed to behave. The temptation to exploit for selfish

purposes institutions possessing great moral prestige is particularly strong. What is more, it is almost a law of history that movements and their institutional expressions should begin with great promise, flower and bear fruit, and then wither and die. The world is full of the monuments of dead nations, cultures, and religions. To say that churches display the same tendencies is only to say that they belong to this world and are composed of real people.

What is truly strange is the power of internal renewal which appears to be at work in the Church. It constantly happens that the Church in a particular place has seemed to be on the point of dissolution and men have begun either to rejoice or to lament at its demise when, often in a quite new way, the Spirit has breathed upon it once more and made its dry bones live. This happened in the life of the old Israel in the Old Testament and it happens even more frequently in the more stable and purposeful setting of the Church, the new Israel. It is true that not all parts of the Church's life show this power at work with equal clarity. Broadly speaking, and for a variety of good and bad reasons, the churches of Eastern Christendom have not shown this characteristic to anything like the same degree as the Protestant and Catholic West, but this tendency does not cease to operate today and we shall have occasion to note its work several times in the course of our discussion.

An eloquent popular preacher, wishing to challenge a Christian audience in London to fulfill their evangelistic responsibilities more effectively, asked them to imagine the kind of progress that the Communists would have made if, like the Christians, they had had the unrivaled opportunity to spread their propaganda in all the parishes of England for over a thousand years. It was a most unrealistic question, for what evidence does Communism provide that it is able to maintain its adherents in a state of pure evangelistic zeal even for a genera-

tion? The strange thing about the Church is not that it grows
old, but that it seems to have discovered the secret of being
born again.

But can a man, or an institution, be born again when they
are old? Nicodemus' bewildered question in the Fourth Gospel, with its obvious reference to the challenge with which the
coming of the Holy Spirit confronted the old Israel, has a peculiar directness when the history of the Church is considered.
When Jesus replies that with men it is impossible, He is asserting what is no more than an ascertainable fact. Neither individuals nor institutions are able to find of themselves the secret
of perpetual youth. Jesus goes on to say that with God all
things are possible. If that is true, and if the Church does reveal, however brokenly, something of this ability, does it
provide more justification than might have appeared at first
sight for the Church's claim to be the instrument of the purpose
and the bearer of the Spirit of the living God? What is clear, at
least, is that the fact that the Church is strange in this sense
constitutes its best claim on the attention of men. To put the
question in the evocative terms of the Bible, is that bush which
appeared to Moses so near the beginning of the story, the bush
which burned and was not consumed, a faithful sign? This is the
fundamental question which must be in the mind of any person who tries to look seriously at the Church.

This is the fundamental question, but that does not mean
that it is the only one. On the contrary, the Church needs to be
looked at from many angles before the material for an answer
to this question itself can become available. The importance of
studying churches in their proper historical setting if we are
not to be misled by superficial impressions has already been
emphasized. It is no less important to look at them not merely
in the light of their official teaching and the claims they make
for themselves, but also in their general social context. History

and the social studies have not yet made the contribution that they are able to make to the understanding of the Church. A great deal of confusion has been caused by the practice of making a sharp distinction between the spheres of secular and ecclesiastical history, as typified by the oft-noted absence of any significant reference to the missionary movement in the *Cambridge Modern History*. There is, of course, a justification for a working distinction between secular and ecclesiastical history, but one must always remember that many aspects of the life of ecclesiastical institutions belong primarily to secular history and that the Church does not exist in a peculiar half-world of its own. Christian study itself demands that churches be subjected to ordinary historical and sociological investigation, certainly with a due recognition of the full character of their distinctiveness as institutions, but with no sense that rude hands are being laid on the ark of the covenant.

Attempts at the realistic assessment of the nature and function of the Church undoubtedly suffer from a tradition of excessive politeness in dealing with these matters. The clergy, like mothers, are sacrosanct in public discussion, whatever may be said about them in private. It would be frivolous not to appreciate the genuine respect which this convention expresses. At the same time, the one public place where such formal restraint is inappropriate is in theological discussion. Theologians of all people should not hesitate to "cast a cold eye" over the churches and, in particular, to consider how far history and present experience justify the more pretentious claims that some of them make for themselves. This is desirable, not in order to keep up with the still fashionable practice of "debunking," nor because there is necessarily a great deal that is discreditable to uncover, but because of the nature of the realities with which we have to deal. The very faith which Christians profess in the divine institutions and commission of the Church demands that they be sober and honest about the achievements of those bodies which are its visible expression. We believe in the Holy Catholic Church, in the words of the Creed, but we do so, not because we believe it has some self-justifying and self-generating power of its own, but only because we believe in God the Father Almighty and in Jesus Christ, His Son our Lord. We shall have to pay a good deal of attention to what is involved in putting things in this order at later stages of this argument. For our present purpose, it is enough to note that it gives to the theologian full freedom to speak about the Church from every angle, in a setting of full responsibility to the Church.

CHAPTER II

Is the Church Necessary?

It is curious how little attention is paid to the significance of the Church in discussions of the truth, or otherwise, of the Christian faith. The Christian faith is normally considered as a way of interpreting life which proves its validity by the fruits which it brings forth in the lives of individuals but not so much by the character of the community it creates. On the contrary, the Church is often treated as an embarrassment to the apologist for the Christian faith, something he has to explain away rather than a means of supporting his claim. The phrase "moral man and immoral society" would seem to apply as much to the relation of the Christian to the common life of the Church as it does to that of the individual to society in general.

This is partly due to the reasons which have already been mentioned, that the achievements of many modern churches are unimpressive and that the life and witness of the churches are bound up so closely with the dominant nations of the West and their way of life. This can be very clearly seen in the attitude of those political and social leaders in Eastern countries, mentioned by John Foster in his book *Why the Church?*,[1] who claim to follow Christian ideals but who will have little or nothing to do with the churches. Another reason, however, is one which can be no less clearly seen in the attitude of many liberally minded people in the Western world. These find it easier to admire Christ and the Christian ideal from a safe distance than to join in fellowship with other people, who may be awkward and personally uncongenial to them, in trying to work out that ideal in practice.

But the matter is more complicated than that. For in Protestant lands, and particularly where there are large churches of what are known as the Free Church type, such as the Methodist, Baptist, and Congregationalist, many active and devoted churchmen are to be found who themselves disparage the Church and give very little theological significance to its existence. Until recently it was a not uncommon thing to hear Protestant preachers explaining to their own congregations from their own pulpits that the Church was a necessary evil and that Jesus clearly never intended to found a Church. It is true that the official teaching of most of these bodies is very different from this. But the attitude is quite widespread and does a great deal to color the approach toward the churches of many people both within and outside them. It is worth asking, therefore, how it has come about.

The extent of the influence of Pietism and the closely related movement of Revivalism on the development of Protestantism in both America and Britain, and through them on the consciousness of large sections of the population of the modern world, has still been inadequately estimated. Pietism, the parent movement, started among such groups as the Mennonites and Moravians in Germany and, partly through their agency but chiefly through Methodism, spread to English-speaking

[1] S. C. M. Press, London, 1954.

lands in the eighteenth and nineteenth centuries. It reacted against the coldness and formalism and intellectualism of post-Reformation religion by a strong emphasis on the warmth and tenderness of the personality of Jesus and on the need for a spontaneous act of conversion as the individual's response to Him. It stimulated a strong sense of fellowship among the members of a particular religious group, but it was a fellowship among those concerned chiefly for the cultivation of the internal life of individuals, the so-called "spiritual life." This was suspicious of institutionalism because it might quench the Spirit and it had little conception of the Church as a permanent society with a divinely ordained form and a public responsibility for the Christian ordering of all parts of the common life of believers. Revivalism, which came after Pietism, represented a much more violent and crude form of the same attitude. Its whole energy was directed toward inducing, and even more toward reinducing, the conversion experience, which it inclined to consider as the end as well as the beginning of the Christian life.

These movements have had the great virtue of possessing terrific evangelistic power. They have produced more new Christians than any other form of church life in the modern world. No churches have a record of expansion more remarkable than that of churches of Methodist and Baptist type in the last hundred and fifty years. But they have produced Christians with a very undeveloped conception of the Church. This is partly because of the emotional and individualistic attitude toward religion which we have seen them to possess. It is also partly because they were either cut off from the rich traditions of older-established churches concerning the relation between the Church and the Gospel or knew those traditions only in most unsympathetic forms. Even those churches with a much fuller conception of the Church, such as the Presbyte-

rian, Episcopalian, Lutheran, and Congregationalist, were influenced by the individualism of these movements and were
not able to restate their doctrines of the Church in a way which
was sufficiently luminous to catch the attention of the fervent,
rootless Christians they produced. The result was that men had
little encouragement to believe that the Church was other than
a large, elaborate, legalistic and rigid organization which
seemed to them to deny the simplicity and power of the Gospel
of Jesus, and they sought to have as little of it as they possibly
could.

The attitude was understandable, and that it should have
arisen was a grave reproach to those who belonged to the more
mature churches. But it is seen in increasingly wide circles today to be dangerously naïve and false to the plain import
of Scripture. It is naïve because spontaneity and simplicity are
not as easily achieved as its exponents supposed. To the extent
to which they were successful, those bodies found themselves
developing into large institutions and facing all the problems
of legalism and formalism and professionalism for which they
reproached other churches. And it is dangerous because the
fact that they imagined that they were free from the possibility
of falling into these dangers made them uncritical in dealing
with them and unable to call on the resources of the Gospel to
overcome them. Methodism, in consequence, often shows
more of the failings of institutionalism than does Episcopalianism.

The fact that these churches overlooked the extent to which
their suspicion of the doctrine of the Church was un-biblical is
curious. Most forms of Pietism—Quakerism is one of the few
exceptions—are religions of the Book. Revivalism, in its modern
form of Fundamentalism, is aggressively so. Yet old-fashioned
Protestantism was remarkably selective in its interpretation of
Scripture and individualistic in the way it handled even the

Is the Church Necessary?

21

passages which it cherished. Thus, to this day, many Fundamentalist preachers find it hard to move very far away from the sixth chapter of Romans, and even that they interpret on their own assumptions. This individualism was taken over by many of the Modernists, who were often the children of pietist or revivalist homes who had reacted against their upbringing. A prominent British modernist preacher once remarked of the words "In sin did my mother conceive me," which occur in Psalm 51, "I should not like to say that of my mother." He was apparently oblivious of the fact that the Psalmist was speaking on behalf of the penitent community of Israel, and that the reference was probably to Eve and the Fall and the weight of the sin of the whole race, in which they were acknowledging their part.

Modern Protestantism, both Conservative and Liberal, has, in fact, shown very little ability to see any relation between its thinking about the community and what the Bible has to say about the Church. This was true, for instance, in the Social Gospel movement, which had much to say about the Kingdom and about society, but curiously little about the Church as the obvious link between the two. Today, however, the renewed conversation with churches of other traditions and the desire for reunion which the Ecumenical Movement has promoted, combined with a great revival of the study of biblical theology, has created a very different situation. Protestantism has become acutely conscious of the doctrine of the Church and of its own deficiencies in this respect. For some, notably Presbyterians and Congregationalists, this has meant a rediscovery of many elements in their own classical teaching which had long been overlooked; but, for all, the recovery of a fuller picture of what the Bible teaches about the Church in relation to God's action in Christ has meant a realization that it is ultimately inadequate to regard the Church only as a necessary evil. It is

part of the Christian reality itself, and the Christian faith makes
little sense without it. It will be the aim of the next four chapters
to show how this conclusion has been reached.

Protestants, however, are not the only Christians in existence,
and there will be many who, if they have kept company with
us thus far, will be increasingly impatient and confused. They
will say that it is hardly surprising that Protestants should raise
the question whether the Church is necessary. If they believed
it to be necessary, they would never have left it, or would seek
to join it. What do I mean by the Church? Surely it must be that
visible society which was founded by our Lord and the apostles
and which has certain clearly defined marks. What point is
there in speaking of the Church or the churches in this loose
and generalized way?

We shall, of course, have occasion to look at Catholic teaching about the Church several times in the course of our argument. Here, however, we may accept its challenge to the extent
of seeking to define more precisely what we mean by the
Church than did our original provisional definition.

Bishop Stephen Neill, in his book *The Christian Society*,[2]
gives six different senses in which the word "Church" is commonly used. First, there is the mystical sense, as the Bride of
Christ, the indefectible exalted Church which cannot err or fail,
sinless as Christ is. This is the sense in which Eastern Orthodoxy
generally speaks of the Church. Secondly, it can refer to the fellowship of all the redeemed in all ages, whose number is known
to God alone, "the invisible Church" of some Protestant thought.
Thirdly, it is the body of all who within history share in God's
covenant of grace, through fellowship within the body, which
is the appointed channel of that grace. This widely held con-
cept is the one which was accepted as a provisional definition
of the Church in the first chapter, leaving in abeyance for the

[2]James Nisbet, London, 1952.

time being the question of where the limits of this body are to be discerned. Fourth, it is used to describe a particular local church, a fellowship of such bodies being called churches. This is what is often held to be the position of churches of Congregationalist type and has the advantage of being very close to New Testament usage. Circumstances have led, however, to a wide extension of this notion of locality in relation to a church, and in modern usage this has been extended to cover the church of a whole nation, "The Church of England" or "Church of Sweden." This, presumably, is Bishop Neill's fifth type, though he does not explicitly say so. Last, the word applies to a denomination, such as the Methodist or Lutheran church.

In different ways, both the Roman Catholic and the Eastern Orthodox churches would assert that they saw no problem in their definition of the meaning of the Church. The Church is that body which holds communion with themselves, and whatever might be the status of individuals outside their fellowship, the institutions in which those individuals hold membership cannot be called churches. Many Anglo-Catholics would share their view, though they would be anxious to assert that their own and other churches claiming true apostolic succession should be accounted among their number. This position is, however, not one which has commended itself to vast numbers of Christians throughout the world. It is impossible to speak without ambiguity of the Church, and there are occasions when we shall use the term in every one of Bishop Neill's six senses, hoping that the context will make the meaning clear.

The nearest we are likely to get to an objective discussion of this matter is by considering the Church as it developed in Scripture and in the history of the early Church. Of course, even here, the presentation of the material will be conditioned by the approach of the writer. The reader does well to remember that the author is a Congregationalist. But it would be equally wrong to suppose that no wide consensus of opinion is discernible among Christians about the nature of the Church. On the contrary, one of the most heartening features of recent theological discussion and spiritual experience has been the emergence of a common viewpoint among Christians of very different ecclesiastical tradition. The richest and deepest book about the life of the apostolic church which has appeared for a generation, *The Common Life in the Body of Christ*,[3] by the Anglo-Catholic monk, Lionel Thornton, received an enthusiastic welcome from representative Free Churchmen. And the conviction is steadily growing among Christians of most denominations in the Ecumenical Movement that when they speak about the Church they are speaking a common language about a common reality. Differences remain, of course, both of principles and of emphasis, especially over familiar controversial matters like episcopacy and the sacraments. But they are now seen in a context of even greater agreement. All churchmen worthy of the name see that their ministry denies the purpose of the body to which they belong if it is not a ministry of reconciliation and a ministry, first of all, to their divided Christian brethren. And all agree that the basis of reconciliation is to be found in Jesus Christ and the Church of Scripture.

[3]Dacre Press, London, 1942.

CHAPTER III

The Old Testament and the Church

The historical root of the Church is in the covenant which Abraham and his children entered into with Yahweh their God. As Mary sings in her "Magnificat," when she knows that she is to give birth to the Messiah, who is to be the fulfillment of the hope of Israel, "He hath holpen Israel his servant, that he might remember mercy (as he spake unto our fathers), toward Abraham and his seed for ever."

It is worth stressing that this is something more than a pleasing poetic fancy. The ground for this assertion is the fact that continuity of experience exists between Abraham and the Church. The story of the movement which reached its fulfillment in the Church had its beginning, as far as our eyes can discern at this distance, in that moment when Abraham felt constrained to obey the voice of another who confronted him and said, "Get thee out of thy country, and from thy kindred and from thy father's house, unto the land which I shall show thee; and I will make of thee a great nation, and I will bless thee, and make thy name great" (Genesis 12:1–2). Everything which happened later appears to have come from that, and if

Christian experience of God is valid, that of Abraham must be held to be valid also.

This is not to say that we are necessarily committed to the acceptance of all the narratives of the Patriarchs as they are told in Genesis, written over in the light of later experience as they are, still less all the ideas of God's nature and action which they portray. What Christians must accept is that, however inadequately it may have been grasped, God did speak a mysterious word of promise to the first fathers of Israel, which prompted them to go in this way rather than that, and in so doing set in train a series of events which led to the Exodus and what followed from it. This, after all, is the meaning of those otherwise pointless stories so familiar from Sunday school, those of Jacob and Esau and Joseph and his brethren and the rest. They are meant to show us the hand of God at work in apparently ordinary stories of fear and jealousy and intrigue and affection, preparing the ground for the maturing of His purpose in His own time.

That purpose becomes much clearer in the great event which followed, the Exodus from Egypt. It is hard to exaggerate the significance which this event, together with the related events of the giving of the Law on Sinai, the sojourn in the wilderness, and the settlement in the Promised Land, had for Israel's understanding of herself. It is only recently that these have received their due measure of attention from critical scholars, but now it is again widely recognized that it was the Exodus and its related events which formed Israel into a conscious community with a definite purpose which set her apart from other nations and gave her a pattern of life which equipped her to fulfill that purpose.

The memory of the great promise to Abraham and the sense of a special guidance which had hung over them in their nomadic days must still have lingered among the Israelites while they lived in Egypt. Otherwise it is hard to see what basis Moses would have had for his appeal. But for all practical purposes, they must have been virtually indistinguishable from the rest of the people held captive in Egypt. That is to say, there is no indication that they were the chosen people. They were part of the masses, the great, anonymous multitudes of humanity. These are the people who have no history, because their life has no apparent purpose. They drift through life, "Living and partly living," and their end is as their beginning. Their lot is that which Job, in his despair, describes as the lot of all men: "Man that is born of woman is of few days and full of trouble. He cometh forth like a flower, and is cut down: He fleeth also as a shadow, and continueth not" (Job 14:1–2). Yet suddenly something happens which makes it all different. A man of strange, ambiguous background is raised up to be their deliverer. We are told, in one of the greatest passages of the Bible, the third chapter of Exodus, that God speaks to him out of a bush which burns and is not consumed, declares His hidden name to him as that of the God of Abraham, Isaac, and Jacob, and commissions him to lead those who are the people of God out of Egypt into a land which He has promised them. This he persuades a half-reluctant people to do and, after mysterious and terrible adventures, the Exodus is accomplished.

The picturesque stories of the Ten Plagues and the Crossing of the Red Sea, which lend themselves so readily to treatment in glorious technicolor, have served to distract a great deal of modern attention from the real miracle of the Exodus, which is the fact that it took place at all. For, whatever the exact details of the story—and they are peculiarly hard to determine at this time of day on the basis of a record which is both stylized and highly colored—it is clear that a great event of an unparalleled nature took place. The Exodus defies all attempts at explanation simply in sociological or psychological terms. Here was a people who were, as their children looking back in humility described them, no people, part of the nameless mass of the proletariat of the Nile delta, who are transformed, relatively suddenly, into the people of God. Those who were in bondage of captivity in Egypt, passably contented with their mediocre lot, are now set on a long and perilous road whose end they cannot see, moving forward under leadership inspired by the conviction of a mighty destiny. They were called out from the multitudes, as the ecclesia of Christ was later called out, to be the instruments of God's revealing purpose.

That this was no mere outbreak of a restless nomadic group who grew tired of agricultural slavery, nor merely another example of the sudden crystallization of a self-assertive national consciousness, is proved by the event which went with the Exodus. They received the Law on Sinai. They were lifted up onto a new plane of moral insight and obligation which marked them off as a people apart from their fellows. More than that, as the tremendous account of the promulgation of the Law in Exodus 19 is at pains to make clear, they do so as a consequence of an intensively vivid experience of the holiness and majesty of God, who is a Power other and greater than themselves. Henceforward, the Covenant that God made with Abraham was indelibly imprinted on the consciousness of Israel because it had vindicated itself in the deliverance from Egypt and the revelation of the Law. When they finally settled in the land which they believed to be the Promised Land, they never allowed themselves or their children to forget these events, and the Covenant was made the center of their life.

The notion of the Covenant is so fundamental to the understanding of the Church that its nature and terms deserve consideration. The other names for the Old Testament and the New Testament themselves are, of course, the Old Covenant and the New Covenant. The fact that, in the experience of the people, the Covenant was so closely linked with the deliverance from Egypt and the giving of the Law made it very clear that in this Covenant the initiative lay with God. It was not an agreement entered into by two parties where each had rights one against the other. The Hebrew word for covenant, *b'rith,* does not mean a bargain, but "something binding," imposed by the stronger on the weaker. The faithful in Israel always saw clearly that the fact of the Covenant was a testimony to God's electing grace rather than to their own righteousness or worth. As the writer of Deuteronomy said long after the time of Moses, "Yahweh did not set his love upon you, nor choose you, because ye were more in number than any people; for ye were the fewest of all peoples" (Deuteronomy 7:6–7). The proper response of man toward it was not self-glorification but humble obedience and the trusting faith which, as St. Paul so frequently insisted, Abraham himself displayed.

This point must be made clear because it has important implications for the Church's understanding of itself. The old Israel did not fail simply because it was under the Law. The essence of the Law, as Jesus constantly emphasized when He quoted Moses against the Pharisees, was the same as the Gospel. It was a declaration of God's loving grace to His people. God had granted them a marvelous deliverance in bringing them from the house of bondage in Egypt, and in token of His renewed covenant with them, He would show them the way to live acceptably to Him and happily with each other in this world. The original content of the Law, which was obviously much simpler and more fundamental than its later elaboration in Leviticus and Numbers, was less sensitive and profound than its restatement in the new law of love of Jesus, but its inspiration was the same, the free grace of a saving God revealing His will to men that they might have life and have it more abundantly.

The old Israel's failure, therefore, did not consist in the fact that she lived by an imperfect Law but by the fact that she so misconceived the nature of that Law as to make it a barrier rather than a road to communion with God. As St. Paul, the Jew who had lived all this out in his own experience, insisted, she had turned the Law from God's ordinance designed to sustain men in grateful obedience to Him into a means by which they could justify themselves in God's sight. They wanted to transform the Covenant into a contract, where they could negotiate as equals with God and boast of its blessings as rights which they had earned, and in doing so they turned it into a curse instead of a blessing. History has proved that the Church is abundantly able to do the same with the New Covenant. In intention, however, the Old Covenant was one of grace, and the sanctified Christian imagination, as it has expressed itself in liturgy and hymn, has not been wrong in seeing the Exodus as the Old Testament type of the Resurrection, and the giving of the Law as the type of Pentecost, and the sojourn in the wilderness as that of the pilgrimage of God's people through an alien world to the Promised Land which is their home.

In view of the criticisms often made of the failings of modern churches, it should be noted that, from the outset, it is never suggested that Israel is a community of the perfect. Some of the later prophets, who stood at a sufficient distance away, idealized the wilderness period as that of Israel's honeymoon with Yahweh, but it does not require a very careful reading of Exodus to note that, even at the time when the great events of the Red Sea and of Sinai must have been vivid in their recollection, they were frequently recalcitrant, defiant, and, not least, skeptical. We are told that they "murmured" against Moses, that they slipped back into open idolatry, and that, when they ran into difficulties, they compared their situation in the wilderness unfavorably with that which they had left in Egypt, and told Moses that the whole enterprise on which he had led them was a wild-goose chase. Cynicism, unbelief, and disobedience have been factors with which the Church has had to reckon from the beginning, and she has always overcome them not by ignoring or denying them but by confronting and overcoming them in faith.

More than that, the events associated with the Exodus so dominated the consciousness of the later Israel that they provided them with one of the strongest assurances they possessed of the reality and grace of God. When they were filled with forebodings about their future, they argued thus with themselves: "What are the most certain facts that we know? We know that God called our fathers and delivered them out of the hand of Pharaoh from Egypt. We know that He gave them the Law through Moses, and that the Law has proved itself to be a lamp unto our feet and light unto our path. We know that He led them miraculously through the wilderness to the Promised Land, where we now dwell. If it were not so, our possession of the Law and our present existence become a monstrous enigma. We cannot deny these facts without denying ourselves." Thus they were able to go on to argue that the God who had established and ratified the Covenant made with their fathers would not be likely to desert them in their present extremity. If they called upon His name in truth, reminding Him of His mighty deeds in the days of old, He would answer them and bless them. Psalms such as 78 and 105–7 present very good examples of this way of thinking.

This is worth noting because, on its own assumptions, a similar line of argument is not invalid for the Church today. It is partly that the historical events which prompted these reflections in the old Israel are also part of the heritage of the New, as the Church recognizes when sermons are preached from them as texts, but it is also that the greater events of the ministry, death, and resurrection of Jesus Christ and the gift of the Spirit carry the same message even more directly. When Christians ask themselves whether there is any future for the Church, that question must not be answered on the level of an assessment of apparent present possibilities. It must be considered in the light of these mighty acts by which God has vindicated His holy name in the past and which provide the ground of the confidence of His people for the future. This is one reason why, as we shall see later, the recollection, or better the re-presentation, in the sense of making present anew, of these saving events is one of the chief characteristics of the Church's worship.

The significance of this line of argument is reinforced when the intensity with which the members of Israel conceived themselves to possess a corporate personality is borne in mind. This is another of those notions, hard for the modern consciousness to grasp, which is yet of cardinal importance for understanding the scriptural conception of the Church. Israel conceived of itself as a spiritual unity. All who belonged to Israel were members one of another to the extent of sharing a common soul. This unity ran through time as well as space. All the past members of Israel were conceived to be simultaneously involved in the deliberations and affairs of the present. This made them consider it quite natural to accredit to Moses books which could not possibly have been written by him and to claim the authority of a great prophet for utterances made by another. The spirit of Moses or the prophet rested upon the author. It was their voice speaking in the present.

It is wrong to think of this notion as necessarily crude and undifferentiated and to go on to claim, as some Old Testament historians have, that the way of progress lay in the movement from this generalized sense of the group to religious individualism. The matter is more complicated than that. It is true that in some of its early manifestations this sense of corporate personality was crude and even barbarous, as the practice of "devoting" a conquered enemy and his possessions shows (Leviticus 27:28). But the way of progress was not toward individualism but toward a richer and more precise idea of corporate personality. The great prophets like Jeremiah and Hosea and the author of Isaiah 40–55 did not set the individual in his distinctiveness over against Israel. They gave a more inward and personal interpretation to what it meant to be Israel. It was the notion of corporate personality which made sense of the idea of the righteous remnant of Israel which would be taken by God as representative of the whole and which, as the song of the suffering servant in Isaiah 53 expressed it, would make atonement for the sins of the people and justify them in God's sight.

No idea is more central to the doctrine of the Church than this. Jesus saw Himself as Israel, the sole representative of the righteous remnant who, through His identification with His people and by His sacrifice, was able to reconstitute the people of God in His Body and to impart to them His righteousness as they were incorporated in Him. Without some understanding of the idea of corporate personality, it is hard to make much sense even of such familiar expressions as "membership of the body of Christ." It is also hard to make much of the other idea, which St. Paul developed, of Christ as the second Adam. In the thought of Israel, Adam was not the first historical man, for whose act of disobedience all the rest of us are made responsible by the arbitrary dictate of a capricious and unjust God; he was the archetypal figure who represents all humanity. The identity between him and us is such that his actions and their consequences are ours also. Christ is the second Adam, the archetypal figure of the new humanity, "the first-born of many brethren," who, as representative of us all, wins salvation for us. "As in Adam all died," therefore, "so in Christ shall all be made alive," and the Church is the first-fruits of this new humanity. In the same way, the notion of the covenant implies that of corporate personality. Abraham's seed are involved in the promise given to their father, and the New Covenant works both prospectively and retrospectively for those who are of one heart and mind with Jesus Christ.

The whole story of Israel in the Old Testament is full of illumination for the Church's understanding of itself, both positively and negatively. There are three other points which are particularly deserving of attention.

First, if Catholics have been disposed to overemphasize the importance of the Priesthood and the Temple for the Church, Protestants have been inclined to underemphasize it. It is wrong to make too sharp a distinction between prophets and priests in ancient Israel, and to side always with the former against the latter. Prophets frequently denounced corruptions and abuses of the temple worship, but they denounced false prophets in even stronger terms. Many of the Psalms prove that there was a tradition of the deepest prophetic spirituality closely associated with the temple worship. And recent scholars have shown how ideas derived from the temple worship have been taken up by the Church to express some of the richest truths of Christian faith.[1] Thus the heart of the temple worship was that of the tabernacling presence of God, typified by the Shekinah cloud which hovered around the ark of the covenant. This is fulfilled in the Christian belief in the indwelling of the Holy Spirit, as it was developed both by St. Paul and St. John.

This does not affect the validity of the second point, that the prophetic tradition represents the main line of the move-

[1] See *The People and the Presence,* by W. J. P. Phythian-Adams (Oxford, 1942).

ment of the Old Testament toward Christ. After all, He Himself regarded it as such. What united the prophets was their
conviction that Israel could cherish no assurance that she would
automatically inherit the promises, no matter how she be-
haved. The only condition of her doing so was ever-renewed
obedience to the living will of God in the changing circumstances of her life. To put her trust in offerings or in regular
attendance at temple worship, or even in looking forward to a
day of the Lord which would vindicate her against her enemies, was to invite God's judgment. As her calling carried with
it special privileges, so it carried special responsibilities. "Thee
only have I known of all the nations of the earth; therefore shall
I visit upon thee double for all thine iniquities." Israel must
see that her only hope is in God and not in herself if she is to
live. That is the point about the Covenant which the great
story of the sacrifice of Isaac makes clear at the very beginning.
Only he who, at the clear behest of God, is prepared to destroy
that which alone carries the human possibility of the Covenant's fulfillment is able to carry forward the Covenant. Israel
must be prepared to die if she is to live. Her traditions, worship,
corporate life, even her apocalyptic expectations, have value
only as they point beyond themselves to God, and if they fail
to do so, they become barriers between men and God. The
message of the prophets clearly receives its fulfillment in the
ministry of Jesus Christ.

Thirdly, the element of universalism is more strongly present
in the Old Testament than might at first appear. Yahweh is not
only the God of Israel but the creator of the heavens and the
earth. Therefore, Israel learns in exile that she is able to know
Him even though she is cut off from His appointed place in the
Temple at Jerusalem. It also means that He has an interest in
peoples other than Israel. The book of Jonah rebukes Israel for
begrudging the possibility of salvation to Nineveh, "wherein

are more than six score thousand souls who know not their right
hand from their left, and also much cattle." Already, the proclamation of the Gospel to the Gentiles, with the judgment
which this carries on the tendencies to religious exclusiveness
within the Church, is implicit in the life of Israel.

It is clear, therefore, that there is more continuity between
the life of the old Israel and the new than has often been acknowledged. The Old Covenant is not one of works but of
grace. It is not denied by Christ but fulfilled. The old Israel
failed not through possessing an inadequate revelation of God
but through its disobedience and its attempt to have God on its
own terms. The long story of that failure, as it reaches its climax
in the rejection of the Messiah, was truly "written for the learn-
ing" of members of the Church, that they might be made "wise
unto salvation."

CHAPTER IV

Jesus and the Church

It has sometimes been suggested, either by sharp critics of the churches or by members of anti-institutional sects like the Quakers, that Jesus never intended to found a Church. The Church, they say, is an invention of His followers, who corrupted the primitive simplicity and purity of His message. Clearly, if by a Church they mean only an elaborate organization of the type represented by the large modern Catholic and Protestant denominations, they are right, but that is a very naïve and superficial conception of what constitutes the substance of the Church. It is true that Jesus proceeded by the method of gathering together a small company of friends in an informal fashion, but there was nothing casual or impressionistic about it. The simple fact that He chose twelve apostles, after the example of the twelve tribes, indicates that He saw His task as nothing less than the reconstitution of the community of Israel, the chosen and covenanted people of God. If it was not Jesus' purpose to found the Church in this radical sense, it is hard to see much meaning in His ministry. He becomes little more than a wise and heroic individual

teacher, whose penetrating observations about the nature of
life make admirable texts for eloquent addresses by popular
preachers who address their personal admirers in solemn
auditoria which they choose to dignify with the name of
churches.

The proof that Jesus intended to found a Church lies, therefore, in the character of His ministry and in the undoubted fact
that the inevitable fruit of that ministry was the foundation of
the Church. Such statements as the famous promise to Peter
that he was the rock on which He would found His Church, on
which Roman Catholics naturally lay such stress, have their
own importance, but in themselves they are not decisive. What
is decisive is the fact that His whole ministry was directed to
the reconstitution of the community of Israel on the basis of a
new covenant between Israel and her God.

It is true that Jesus speaks more of the Kingdom than of the
Church, and that that Kingdom is an eschatological reality;
that is to say, a present power in man's midst through His
Spirit but not finally realizable until He comes again to gather
all things to Himself. But that does not mean that the necessity
of founding a Church is ruled out; it simply defines the nature
of that Church. It is the community of those who live here and
now, in this sinful present age, in the light and by the power of
the final consummation of all things in Christ. It is the community of the interval between His first and second coming.
His preaching is directed to the reconstitution of Israel in
the light of the fulfillment of the Kingdom. His followers are the
little flock to whom it is the Father's good pleasure to give the
Kingdom. His ethical teaching is directed to the nucleus of
the new Israel and it presupposes that His Spirit will be present
in their midst to show them His will and to enable them to
carry it out. It has not been sufficiently noted that this teaching is directed primarily to the community and not to isolated

individuals. The same emphasis on the community is shown in His acceptance of the title of Messiah and by His choosing of the Twelve. They are representatives of the twelve tribes of Israel, the ideal number of the people of God, and it is with them that the new Covenant in His blood is inaugurated at the Last Supper. If this interpretation is wrong, we are faced with the alternative that the title "the New Covenant," which gives its title to the literature which testifies to the Gospel of Christ, was misleading and that, as soon as He left them, His closest followers began, with the utmost sacrificial conviction, to misunderstand and misrepresent Him.

What is more, a great deal of Jesus' teaching was taken up with trying to make clear the nature of the true Israel and with rebuking those who had the responsibility for leading the people for their failure to see and to express that nature. This is most obviously done in the great debate between Jesus and the Pharisees, which takes up a surprisingly large amount of the Gospel narrative, and which is often present as the background of many sayings, parables, and incidents where Israel is not directly mentioned. His charge against them was not that they were so attached to the old Law that they could not recognize a new and better teaching when it came their way; it was that they had misinterpreted the inner meaning of the old Law itself, so that they had led their fellows astray with "traditions of men" and could not see in His teaching the fulfillment of that after which the old Law had been imperfectly striving. They had put last things first and had lost sight of that fundamental love of God and neighbors on which "hang all the law and the prophets," and their scrupulosity and formalism were the more heinous because they were exercised in the name of a faith which was the reverse of these things.

This is shown not only in such incidents and stories as those dealing with Sabbath observance and ritual washings, and in

the complaints about His mixing with publicans and sinners,
but also in those many parables whose precise meaning is often
overlooked in these days. Familiar parables like the Good
Samaritan and the Prodigal Son have a universal message, but
their primary reference is to Israel's misconception of her true
vocation. Both attack the notion that Israel held her position
as God's chosen people by right and could regard herself as
a remnant saved out of the world which could take pride in its
privileged position and stand upon its dignity. Her mission can
be fulfilled only as a saving remnant, which moves out among
men in self-forgetting service of the will of God. A Samaritan
who does the true works of the Law is a more faithful heir of
the Covenant than even a priest or a Levite, and the man who
is in desperate need of help knows the inner meaning of the
law better than the scribe who is proud of his powers of interpretation. His need teaches him his true state before God
and he does not have to ask subtle questions as to who his
neighbor is. In the same way, it is a complete misunderstanding
of his position for the elder son, to whom the parable of the
Prodigal Son is primarily addressed, to begrudge a welcome
to the returned prodigal in his father's house. It proves that he
is more concerned with his own rights and privileges as a member of Israel than with doing the true work of Israel, the servant of the Lord, which is going out to seek and save that which
is lost and rejoicing when it is found.

The issue between Jesus and the leaders of the Jews is much
more than that between religious individualism and institutionalism or between the creative pioneer and the defender of
vested interest. To see it in those terms, as idealistic Christian
reformers are apt to do, is unduly to simplify the issue and to
be confirmed in the self-righteousness for which Jesus denounced the Jews. For when it is stated in those terms, it is
not too difficult for men to identify their own interests with

those of Jesus, to assume, for example, especially if they are
not churchgoers, that in the story of the Good Samaritan they
would naturally have the part of the Samaritan rather than
that of the priest or the Levite. But the issue was deeper and
sharper than that. It was one concerning the way in which men
can be justified in God's sight. They believed that it was their
membership of Israel which justified them in God's sight and
that it was their zeal for the Law which justified them as members of Israel. They failed to see, as Abraham saw and as Paul,
the converted Pharisee, was finally made to see, that it is faith
in the gracious promise of God alone which justifies men in
His sight and makes them heirs of the Covenant.

If anything is clear from the New Testament, it is that it
should be the mark of the community of Christ's people that
they are vigilant to avoid the errors of the Scribes and Pharisees
and that they are aware of how infinitely subtle and insidious
those errors are. Part of the purpose of the strange divine
economy of salvation in the calling, disciplining, and final rejection of the old Israel was to placard once for all before men
the fact that the chief barrier which separated them from God
was their own pride. That pride is more operative in the religious realm than anywhere else. Religion itself is not necessarily, as men widely believe today, "a good thing." Like every
other human activity, it also needs to be redeemed by God's
grace, because pride can insert itself even into the heart of a
man who proclaims that he owes all to Christ. The Church,
of all bodies, must "take heed and beware of the leaven of the
Pharisees and Sadducees" (Matthew 16:6). It is one of the
main objections of Protestantism against Roman Catholicism
that it does little to safeguard itself against this fundamental
danger, and Rome has never given an adequate answer. But
Protestants do well to remember here, in particular, what
Jesus said to the Pharisees themselves about motes and beams.

This is the vocational temptation of all churches, and loudly to trumpet one's anti-Pharisaism is the reverse of an effective safeguard against its dangers.

The inescapability of this temptation does not mean, however, that the attempt to give an institutional form to the Church must be rejected. It means only that the Church must have the clearest possible understanding of what membership of the new Israel means and that it must try to express it in its institutional form. It means that the Church can exist as Christ's Body only in the form of a servant. This, again, is one of the main themes of the Gospels. There can be little doubt that Jesus defined His mission in terms of the song of the suffering servant in Isaiah 53, and the contrast between Him and the rulers in Israel in this respect is constantly brought out. It receives its most moving expression in the account, in the Fourth Gospel, of the great acted parable of the washing of the disciples' feet. "Ye call me Master and Lord; and ye say well, for so I am. If I, then, the Lord and Master, have washed your feet, ye also ought to wash one another's feet. For I have given you an example, that ye also should do as I have done unto you. Verily, verily, I say unto you, a servant is not greater than his Lord; neither one that is sent greater than he that sent him" (John 13:13–16).

The distinctiveness of the apostolic office is also defined in terms of service. After the incident of the attempt of the sons of Zebedee to seek pre-eminence, He calls His disciples together and says, "Ye know that they which are accounted to rule over the Gentiles lord it over them; and their great ones exercise authority over them. But it is not so among you; but whosoever would become great among you, shall be your minister; and whosoever would be first among you, shall be servant of all. For verily the Son of Man came not to be ministered unto, but to minister and to give his life a ransom for many" (Mark 10:42–45).

This is driven home with peculiar sharpness in the account of the calling and training of the Twelve and, in particular, in the story of Peter. The apostles are the nucleus of the new Israel, the twelve elders who represent the whole people. Yet it is Judas, one of the twelve, who betrays Jesus, and the plan of betrayal is in operation even when he dips his hand in the bowl during the Last Supper. What is more, it is Peter, the man who made the great confession of faith in Christ's messiahship which evoked the response that it was on the rock of this faith that the Church would be built, who denied Him in the most spectacular and decisive way when the great crisis came. As Cyril of Alexandria observed long ago, the chief primacy which Peter was given in the New Testament was a primacy in denial of his Lord.

It is important to remember that the group of disciples whom Jesus gathered round Him during His earthly ministry were not yet properly constituted as the Church. They became that only after His death, resurrection, and ascension, when the Spirit descended upon them. These mighty events constituted the Church of the New Testament, just as the Exodus and the Law and the tabernacling presence in the Ark constituted the community of Israel in the Old. It was only when He who was the true Israel had bridged the gulf between God and mankind, had demonstrated the victorious power of God over sin, and had borne our mortal natures back to the Father's presence with Him, covered with His righteousness, that the work was complete which inaugurated the new community of God's people and released His Spirit to dwell in their midst.

This is worth pondering upon because it explains the present form of the Church, especially when it assembles itself together for that worship which provides the means by which it lives. First, the new Israel must be brought in by His death. Only thus can the full magnitude of the human rebellion against God be made manifest. The judgment on sin is nothing less than death. That inevitably follows if God is God and if sin is the attempt of man to set himself up as an independent person in defiance of God. The new Israel cannot live unless it sees that, apart from Christ, it is doomed to death and that it cannot hold fellowship with Christ unless it is conformed to His death. It must share with Him the fellowship of His sufferings, as He bears the burden of the sin of the world. The Church must have this attitude whether it experiences material prosperity or adversity, and it must display it in its prayer, in its identification with the cause of all who are in need, and in its service.

Secondly, the true Israel is brought into being through His resurrection. By itself, the death would have been, not merely negation, but tragedy. It would have denied the Covenant made with Israel. Jesus would have gone the way of all flesh, and instead of being the temple of His Body, the apostolic community would have been the sepulcher in which His bitter memory lay hidden. The fact that the Church exists is the most convincing proof of the reality of the resurrection. Unless God had shown in a way which was convincing to the apostles that Christ was stronger than death and that His sacrificial death was not the end of all their hopes but the beginning of a new era, it is inconceivable that the Church could ever have come into being.

Thirdly, the true Israel is brought into being by the ascension. This is a side of the Christian story which has received comparatively little attention in recent times, partly because the way in which it is told raises difficulties for modern minds. These difficulties, which arise chiefly because the story is told in terms of the cosmology of the ancient world, which believed

that heaven was a particular place in the upper air, are real, but
they should not prevent us from acknowledging the central
importance and the logical necessity of the ascension in the
revelation. This is made clear in the great passage in Ephesians
which describes the gifts bestowed by the ascended Christ upon
His Church: "Wherefore he saith, When he ascended on high,
he led captivity captive and gave gifts to men. (Now this
ascended, what is it but that he also descended into the lower
parts of the earth? He that descended is the same also that
ascended from above the heavens, that he might fill all things"
(4:8–9). This filling of all things by Christ as He ascends to
the Father, which is expounded in the first chapter of Ephesians, is what makes possible His release of the Spirit to men,
which constitutes the reality of the Church.

To envisage its physical and psychological manifestations in
terms which carry meaning for us today is peculiarly hard,
but the grandeur and scope of the conception of the ascension and its related events held by the Early Church is un-
mistakable. The disciples on whom the Holy Spirit descended
at Pentecost firmly believed that their Lord, Jesus Christ, had
appeared to them alive for a limited period, which they stated,
perhaps for symbolic reasons, to have been forty days, and that
He then gave them to understand that He would appear to
them in that form no more. His risen and glorified body must
return to His Father, from whom He had come.

The discourses to the disciples in the later chapters of the
Fourth Gospel, which were almost certainly written as an interpretation of His teaching in the light of its issue in events,
explain that it was necessary that He go away, because only
thus could He prepare a place for them that they might be with
Him (John 14:3). The implication of this is that He should
take with Him the humanity which He assumed in His incarnation into the presence of the Father, who is the source and

eternal fulfillment of all life. He takes it, that is to say, to the place where it is no longer tied down by the limitations of time and space, as it was in the days of His flesh. He dwells eternally at the Father's right hand once more, the One through whom all things hold together (Colossians 1:17). But for His work of salvation to be complete, it was necessary that it should be set in the context of the whole universe. As He emptied Himself of His divine majesty to become man, so He must be filled again with all the fullness of God, but this time He does so bearing His broken, crucified manhood with Him, that through Him, we might share in His eternal life (Ephesians 2:5–11).

It was this which the early Church had in mind when it spoke of Him as ascending far above all heavens, that He might fill all things. We cannot think as easily as they did in terms of an ever-expanding spiritual body, subduing all the demons, "the principalities and powers," which were believed to inhabit the upper air, but what they were trying to express is of the utmost importance for the Church's present understanding of itself. They were trying to say that since His physical presence was withdrawn from them, His spiritual presence is now universally available. His influence is no longer limited to one human life nor even solely to one religious tradition. No one need be debarred from touching Him and knowing His healing power because of the press of those about Him. All who call upon the name of the Lord can now be saved because His writ runs through the whole universe. No power is strong enough permanently to resist Him. And His nature and work are such that we see that their influence spreads backward through time as well as forward. There is no escape from the ubiquity of His forgiving love. The proof of the reality of this assurance is not the warmth of the memory of Jesus which men try to retain by gazing up into heaven after the cloud has received Him from their sight (Acts 1:9–11). It is the active presence in the midst of the Spirit, the promised Comforter, Fortifier, Guide, who breaks the bonds of Israel after the flesh and makes men speak of the wonderful works of God, each in his own language. The experience of the Spirit is universal and meets men at the deepest level of their common humanity, and it testifies to the reigning power of the risen and ascended Christ.

The work of Christ in the incarnation, the cross, the resurrection, and the ascension is inseparably bound up with the descent of the Spirit and the founding of the apostolic Church. So far is it from being the case that there is doubt as to whether Jesus founded a Church that it has to be said that the work of Christ is meaningless without the Church and the Church is unintelligible without reference to that work. The different parts of the Gospel cannot be dissociated from each other to suit an arbitrary modern fancy. It was not the Teacher of Galilee, and certainly not that misleading, sentimentalized image of the Teacher of Galilee which has been made the object of devotion in popular Protestantism, who founded the Church. It was the risen and glorified Christ, whom the Teacher of Galilee became. Men cannot claim to belong to the Church until they know that Christ in the Spirit whom He has sent to represent Him and who gives to them that unity which binds them to Him and to one another.

CHAPTER V

The Life of the Apostolic Church

The apostolic community remained in being as one fellowship after the resurrection and the ascension. They knew that they were intended to be together and that, although their destiny was not yet visible, God had great work for them to do. What this work was became clear when the Spirit descended upon them at Pentecost. This event, which appears to have been a specific corporate experience of tremendous power, marks the founding of the Church as an organized community in the world. They were lifted up ecstatically to a new plane of being, speaking with tongues and miraculously being able to understand each other, but it was obvious from the outset that this was more than another outbreak of violent and contagious religious emotion. Something happened at Pentecost which permanently altered the structure of their lives. They quickly settled down to a joyful and responsible common life together and were able to give a coherent and satisfying account of what had overtaken them. Peter, after all, rebutted the charge that they were merely drunken on the day of Pentecost itself. Once they had time to meditate upon it, they saw the coming of the Spirit as the logical fulfillment of all that had gone before, and the Spirit fulfilled the office of which the writer of the Fourth Gospel later spoke, that of guiding them into the truth and bringing back into their consciousness in a new light all that Jesus had said and done when He was on earth. They now believed that they possessed the key to understanding the meaning of the work of Jesus and were ready to fulfill His commission and proclaim His gospel to men.

The records of the first sermons of the Church, as they are recorded in the early chapters of the book of Acts, are primary documents for understanding the attitude of the first Christians toward the Church as well as toward the Gospel. Their main features, as C. H. Dodd has shown in his well-known book, *The Apostolic Preaching and Its Developments,* represent the outlines of a message which was common to the whole apostolic community. The great prophecies of the Old Testament had been fulfilled. Christ had come to inaugurate the promised New Age. He was born of the seed of David. He died, according to the Scriptures, to deliver us from bondage to this present evil dispensation. He was buried and the third day He rose again, also according to the Scriptures. Finally, they declared, He is now exalted to the right hand of God, as Lord over the quick and the dead, and He will come again as Judge and Saviour of men.

Superficially, there seems to be little in this kind of preaching which would be likely to turn the world upside down today. Most modern hearers would probably find themselves bewildered by it. To those who listened to it against the background of the life and expectation of the old Israel, however, it was startling and challenging. It meant nothing less than that God had vindicated Jesus' claim to be the Messiah of Israel and that henceforward membership of Israel could be found in the community of His Spirit. If those who belonged to Israel after the flesh wished to stand justified at the last day, they must repent and be baptized in the name of this crucified Messiah. It is hard to conceive of a message which would have carried a more disturbing challenge than that to those who first heard it.

At first the members of the apostolic community seem to have remained within Judaism, behaving almost as a newly formed Jewish sect might behave, lacking only a synagogue of their own. They joined in the worship of the Temple and frequented synagogues in Jerusalem and Damascus. But it quickly became clear that this was only on the periphery of their new life. Their life had now a new center, in the risen Christ and His presence in the Spirit, through the means of communion which He had appointed. They continued steadfastly "in the apostles' teaching, in the breaking of bread and the prayers." It also followed that the interpretation put upon what took place in the Temple and the synagogues by those Jews who did not accept Christ was different from theirs and that the basis of fellowship between them was progressively weakened. More than that, when they discovered that there were people who did not belong to the old Israel but who were prepared to receive Jesus as Messiah, they could see no reason why they should not enjoy full communion with them as members of the new Israel. The consequence was that, after the death of Stephen, which appears to have occasioned the decisive break between the Church and the Jews and to have led to the departure of many members of the Church from Jerusalem, the mission to the Gentiles began.

It was probably at about this time that the Christian community began to receive its distinctive name. The word "ecclesia" was a somewhat colorless term used in Greek to describe a civic assembly summoned by a herald to a public place to discuss specific business. In the New Testament, however, it is almost certainly a translation of the Hebrew word *Qahal,* the congregation of Israel, God's people gathered together before Him. The ecclesia in a particular place would be understood, therefore, as the embodiment of the people of God, called out by Him for the fulfillment of His public purpose for mankind, a purpose which included both Jews and Gentiles.

That Gentiles should have been so quickly admitted to the Church is one of the most striking indications that with the coming of Christ a new, creative power had appeared in the world. It proved that the people of God now possessed that quality of self-transcendence which only a few prophetic souls had previously seen to be inherent in the nature of their calling. The early Church believed that they had received a commission from the risen Lord to preach the Gospel to all peoples and to gather them into the fellowship of His Church. The attractive suggestion has been made that the form of the commission in Mark, "Go ye and preach the Gospel to the whole creation," might be translated, "Go ye and preach the Gospel ecumenically." That would imply that the Gospel was not merely a message for all men but also for the whole span of existence. In the same way, when Peter had his vision of the edible creatures and was told, "What God hath cleansed, make thou not common" (Acts 10:15), he was also realizing that Christ's commission had a universal scope.

When it is remembered how deeply embedded in the minds of the first Christians was the notion of an exclusive covenant between God and the Jewish people, it is remarkable how they were able to accept this with such comparatively slight difficulty and tension. Even the "Jerusalem authorities," with whom Paul and Peter were frequently in dispute, never doubted the right of Gentiles to belong to the Church. There were, as we have seen, universalistic passages in the Old Testament to which appeal could be made, as Paul and Barnabas did in Antioch of Pisidia (Acts 13:47), but they had been effectively overlaid in the later consciousness of Judaism and their implication had always been that other nations would obey the Law.

It is, perhaps, not surprising that the man who understood most fully the significance of the admission of the Gentiles into the Church should be the man who knew best what it meant to be a member of the old Israel, the apostle Paul. Once again, Ephesians may be invoked. It is debatable whether Paul was its actual author, but it is clearly Pauline in inspiration. After the great outpouring of the first chapter, which places the redemptive work of Christ in the setting of God's eternal purpose running through all time and all creation, it goes on, in the second chapter, to remind the Gentiles that all the great promises of God to Israel belong to them as well as to the Jews. Indeed, the old distinction between Jews and Gentiles no longer applies. They both have access by the same Spirit unto the Father. They are now, therefore, no more strangers and foreigners, but fellow-citizens with the saints and of the household of God. Saints, of course, are not necessarily individuals of outstanding holiness, but members of the people of God and, according to an ingenious recent suggestion, the term may mean specifically the Jewish Christian community. Jews and Gentiles are now together a holy temple in the Lord, a habitation of God through the Spirit. The differences between them have not been ignored, which might only mean that they would reassert themselves on a deeper level, but have been resolved in the unity of the body of Christ. The brotherhood of men is not a natural fact. It is achieved only through the working of supernatural grace, known in its fullness only in the Father's House, the home of all men.

The chief lesson of the admission of Gentiles to the Church

to all future generations of churchmen is obvious enough, although it is one which we always find it particularly hard to learn. Differences of former creed and race and education and station are of secondary importance as compared with the unity of the Spirit. The Church exists to shed abroad Christ's reconciling grace among men who are divided from each other, and denies its very nature when it sets arbitrary limits to the sphere of that grace. But it has another lesson, which is less obvious but hardly less important. The commission to the Gentiles, as Paul shows so vividly in the Epistle to the Galatians, is the charter of the freedom of the Christian man.

This freedom is different from what is known in these days as "religious liberty," although it bears some relation to it. It is the ability to think and act responsibly according to an internal principle of conduct, the law of divine charity, which does not need to be constricted by those rules and regulations which are appropriate to mankind before it has attained its majority. The words of Peter's vision already quoted, "What God hath cleansed, make thou not common," emphasize another side of the same truth. The Christian need not fear that he will stray into situations so remote from the divine influence that it is impossible for him to discover God's will. He is able to respond to the complexity of life along its whole range because He knows that the Spirit is able to guide him into all the truth. The whole universe is the theater of God's glory, and there is no nook or cranny in it where His writ does not run. "Christ has filled all things and all things are put in subjection under His feet and He has been given to be head over all to the Church, which is His body, the fulness of Him that filleth all in all" (Ephesians 1:22–23).

To the extent to which the Church took this conviction seriously, it was inevitable that it should come into direct confrontation with those who held power in this world, and in

particular with the State. In New Testament times the attitude
of the State toward the Church was one of suspicious neutrality,
which quickly turned to persecution. But it was not long as
history goes, however, before the possibility emerged of the
power of the State itself becoming subdued to that of the
Gospel. This took place formally when the Emperor Constan-
tine acknowledged the Christian faith. This has often been
taken to indicate the corruption of the Church by worldliness.
It is certainly true that for the Church to have dealings with
the State is always a difficult and dangerous enterprise, and
the kind of relationship into which it finally entered with the
Empire left much to be desired. But it is most superficial to
regard that as the source of corruption in the life of the Church.
The possibility of worldly corruption was present in the Church
from the beginning, and it quickly became actualized, as the
Epistles to the Corinthians demonstrate. To assume that the
powers of the State can never be subdued by the Gospel is
to limit the universal nature of the Christian claim. It is to
refuse to believe that the kingdoms of this world can ever become the kingdoms of our God and of His Christ. Even if it be
agreed that that happy consummation awaits the second coming of Christ, it is still possible for states to show an awareness
of that high destiny in their present conduct and behave themselves accordingly. That Christian men should someday rule
the State and the other great institutions of secular society, such
as universities, was implied in preaching the Gospel "in an
ecumenical way," to Gentiles as well as Jews. This must be
borne in mind when we consider later the relation of the
churches to the State and secular society today.

Another outstanding characteristic of the early Christian
community was closely related to its conviction of the univer-
sality of the Christian claim, and that was its unity. The Gospel
is, in its essence, a message of reconciliation between God and

man, and hence between men and each other. The unity of the
Spirit is a constant theme of apostolic writing. All had been
baptized into the same Spirit, and by that Spirit they walked.
Or, to put the same point in another way, their unity derived
from their common membership of a body of which Christ was
the Head. This notion has its roots deep in the thought of Israel.
The Messiah and His elect were always thought of as inseparably united, and they could think of no reality which did not
have its concrete embodiment. The Church was, therefore,
the embodiment of Christ, through the indwelling Spirit, although it was this in a form appropriate to that of the Incarnation; that is, in the form of a servant. The members of the
Body express the Spirit of Christ to each other by their mutual
care and service of each other, in the co-inherence of the Body.
There are differences of gift and function among the members,
but none is superior in dignity to the rest, and all are necessary.
Whatever differences may exist, the way of charity, which is
also the way of unity, is open to all. The hymn to love in I
Corinthians 13 follows on directly from the twelfth chapter,
in which this idea of mutual dependence is expressed. It is not
often seen, in circles where I Corinthians 13 is much admired
as an isolated passage, how inseparably linked that idea of love
is to the mutual dependence of members in the body of Christ.

This, of course, is not the whole truth about the relation of
Christ to the Church. If the Old Testament idea of the solidarity of the Messiah with His elect was present in the mind of
Paul when he spoke of Christ as the head of the body, the
other Old Testament idea of the sovereignty of God was not
likely to be absent. Christ is also head, therefore, in the other
sense. He is the controlling and dominating power in the
Church's life, its mind who directs the many members according to His will. The relation between Christ and His Church is
of the closest, but the two are never indistinguishable. Christ

remains the master in His own house and is always free to take
action against disobedient members.

The thought of the directing influence of Christ comes out in
Paul's other favorite metaphor, that of the Church as the bride
of Christ. "Wives, submit yourselves unto your own husbands
as unto the Lord. For the husband is the head of the wife even
as Christ is the head of the Church; and He is the Saviour of
the Body. Therefore, as the Church is subject unto Christ, so
let the wives be to their husbands in everything" (Ephesians
5:22–23). The metaphors are transposed so frequently and
swiftly that it is hard to fasten on the precise meaning of this
passage. He seems to be speaking equally of the relation between Christ and the Church and that between husbands and
wives, and to be using each to throw light on the other. Perhaps
it is worth observing that the writer is not advocating a dictatorship over the wife by the husband, as some have imagined.
Against the background of the ancient world, this chapter is a
landmark in the emancipation of women, because the relationship between husband and wife is given a dignity and spirituality comparable to that between Christ and His Church.
Uncertain though the precise meaning of this passage may be,
one thing is clear. The initiative and the ultimate responsibility for the well-being of the Church rests with Christ, harmo-
niously fused in a relationship of the deepest personal intimacy
which is never complete identification.

The other outstanding New Testament metaphors of the
Church underline the same truth. The Church is a building,
in which God dwells as He previously dwelt in the Temple.
Through Christ's death and resurrection a new temple has
been built, even the temple of His body, indwelt and knit together by the Holy Spirit. At other times each member is
thought of as a stone in the building, held together by Christ,
who is the cornerstone. The purpose of the cornerstone is to

hold two walls together and to support the superstructure. Without Christ, therefore, the whole building of the Church would collapse. It is the same with the metaphor of the vine, which is developed so richly in John 15: "As the branch cannot bear fruit of itself, except it abide in the vine: no more can ye, except ye abide in me."

The third great emphasis of the apostolic teaching is upon the Church as the final home of all men. Here, once more, the key passage is the tremendous first chapter of Ephesians: "That ye may know what is the hope of his calling, what the riches of the glory of his inheritance in the saints, and what the exceeding greatness of his power to us-ward who believe, according to the strength of his might which he wrought in Christ, when he raised him from the dead, and made him to sit at his right hand in the heavenly places, far above all rule and authority and power and dominion, and every name that is named, not only in this age, but also in that which is to come; and he put all things in subjection under his feet, and gave him to be head over all things to the Church, which is his body, the fulness of him that filleth all in all" (Ephesians 1:18–23; see also Colossians 1:15–20).

As we have seen, this presupposes a cosmology different from our own, but it is far from being a piece of heady and verbose rhetoric. It follows on from the argument of the first half of the chapter, which has described the eternal purpose of God in the calling of His people, and it is the logical consequence of belief in the resurrection. If Christ has truly conquered sin and death and we have become members of His body, nothing less than what this passage describes is our ultimate destiny. The mighty power which creates and sustains all things is available for us to draw upon, and the powers of the age to come, when God shall be all in all, can lead us to that joyful consummation. Christ is no private lord of particular individuals or groups. He

is the inner meaning of all things. The theme of this passage
is the same, although the language is different, as that of the
prologue to the Fourth Gospel. That such a notion is hard for
our minds to grasp is no reason for neglecting it.[1] Without it,
as we shall see, it is hard to make much sense of such matters
as the Church's teaching concerning baptism or its approach to
the life of secular society.

It is partly because the apostolic Church saw the reign of
Christ as a cosmic reign that it was dominated by eschatological forms of thought. The eschatological teaching of the New
Testament has been a frequent subject of discussion in theological circles recently, but, as those preparing for the Evanston
Assembly of the World Council of Churches on "Christ the
Hope of the World" discovered, widespread suspicion and misunderstanding of it exists even among Christians, partly because of its misuse by sects which proclaim a crude apocalyptic
millenarianism. The Last Things of which New Testament
eschatology speaks are not merely the events connected with
the end of the world, as that is conceived in the popular imagination. The term refers chiefly to the ultimate realities, those
things which abide when all else has passed away and which
are the fulfillment of what is most vivid and real in this present
life.

The earliest preaching of the Church was, to use C. H.
Dodd's famous phrase, "realized eschatology," or, to use a term
upon which he has recently looked not unkindly, "inaugurated
eschatology." The men of the New Testament thought of history as a series of aeons or ages where different spiritual powers
ruled. We live "in this present age," which is under sentence of
death and is passing away to nothingness. But in Christ "the
powers of the age to come," the age of His final reign in blessed-

---

[1]*The Cosmic Christ,* by Allan Galloway (James Nisbet, London, 1951),
will help to clarify some of these ideas.

ness and peace, have become present in our midst. When He said, "The Kingdom is within you," He did not mean simply that His kingdom was internal and spiritual. He was speaking eschatologically of His kingly rule being actual and manifest in our midst here and now. To put it in a way which may be more readily intelligible today, the vision of the risen Christ in the Spirit, which we have seen to be constitutive of the Church, is a vision of the final realities. We see that He is the One who bears and expresses the decisive truth about life's meaning and destiny, the first and the last and the living one, who holds "the keys of death and of hell" (Revelation 1:18).

The same truth is expressed in the Fourth Gospel, when it speaks of Christ as bringing eternal life. This is not merely the promise of bliss hereafter, but a reality which we experience as "more abundant life" here and now. There is no decisive difference between the teaching of the Fourth Gospel and the Synoptic Gospels in this respect, despite the arguments of those who say that the eschatological expectation of the early Church had faded into the background by the time the Fourth Gospel was written. The initial tendency of the Church was to think of the end in terms which were too strictly chronological, although that may have been their intensive way of expressing how it should be taken into all calculations concerning Christian conduct here and now. When they found that the second coming was not likely to take place in their own lifetime, however, they were able to express the same truth in other terms without serious difficulty, which suggests that they saw that the truth of Christ's teaching about the end did not depend on a belief in the chronological imminence of His second coming.

They were, in fact, able to give the most positive interpretation to the significance of the continuing life of the people of God in this world, which is something those sects which con-

centrate morbidly on the end of the world today are rarely
able to do. Christians have a vision of the end in the risen and
victorious Christ. But that victory is not yet decisively manifest.
A space and a time have been given to men in which to recognize for themselves that He is victor and to conform their lives
to that fact. This is the time of the Lord's patience. To say it is
a very short time indeed, as the early Paul did, is not necessarily
false to the urgency of the decision with which Christ confronts men. The task of the people of God is to live in the light
and by the power of that final victory of Christ in ever-renewed
specific acts of obedience by which the power of "this present
age" is overcome. Meanwhile, they have peace with God
through the indwelling Spirit, which is the earnest, the first
installment, of their final inheritance.

This attitude is the reverse of escapist. The glory of the world
to come is not offered to Christians as compensation for the
frustrations and miseries of the present, as "pie in the sky when
you die." On the contrary, as Romans 12:1–2 shows, the early
Church derived its ethical zeal and its zest for living from its
eschatological expectation, "Be ye not fashioned according to
this present age; but be ye transformed by the renewing of
your mind, that ye may prove what is the good and acceptable
and perfect will of God." This is a development of the familiar
exhortation to live in this world but not to be of it. That does
not mean that we are to be unworldly in the sense of being
uninterested in what goes on around us and ignorant of the
possibilities both of good and of evil which our present life con-
tains. It means to live in this life as those who are not under
sentence of death, like those who are conformed to this present
aeon, but as those who know that they have an eternal home,
where truth and goodness and beauty dwell without corruption, and that these realities are stronger than the error and
evil and ugliness which beset us. The constant advice to live

as children of the light and of the day bears the same interpretation. The day in question is the day of the Lord, when He shall gather all things in glory to Himself. The purpose of the worship of the Church, of the means of grace as they are called, is to renew our mind by refreshing our vision of the end in Christ and giving us light for our path through this world from its radiance. How this is worked out in relation to preaching and sacraments and expressed in the walk and conversation of the Church will be the theme of succeeding chapters. What must be emphasized from the outset is that these long-neglected ideas are not pious and eccentric fancies but are integral to the Church's understanding of its most fundamental activities.

CHAPTER VI

Jesus Christ as the Life of the Church

Scripture shows that what constitutes the Church as the Church is the presence in its midst of God through the living Christ in the fellowship of the Spirit. The existence of the Church arises directly out of the ministry of Jesus Christ. *Ubi Christus, ibi ecclesia.* The Church is not a general society for the promotion of religion, nor is it a device for giving dignity and idealism to the nation on its own secular assumptions. It arose only because Jesus Christ inaugurated a new Israel as a judgment upon and fulfillment of the old, and it continues in being only because His life is still present in the midst as the Spirit. Its faith is that He will sustain His people until all things reach their ultimate fulfillment in Him.

It is common ground among all Christians that the Church owes its foundation to Jesus Christ and that it continues in existence because His Spirit animates it. This is worth noting because outside critics are always disposed to exaggerate the differences between churches. Miss Dorothy Sayers once remarked that when she wrote books and pamphlets about the Christian faith she tried never to write anything which was not acceptable to the Church of England, the Roman Catholic Church, and the Orthodox churches of the East, and that when she did so, she was surprised by the number of appreciative letters which came from members of the Free churches. Serious differences arise between the churches about the way in which Jesus Christ makes Himself known to His people. It will be obvious in what follows that I write from the point of view of Reformed Protestantism and as a Congregationalist. That does not mean, however, that I necessarily believe that the traditional position of my own church is right in every particular or that I cannot see how members of other churches have reached different conclusions from those of my own. The rise of the Ecumenical Movement, as we have seen, has made members of most churches see both the relativity of many of their distinctive beliefs and the extent to which the New Testament conception of the Church exposes the limitations of all church traditions.

Modern orthodox Protestantism is at one with all forms of Catholicism in saying that the Church knows Jesus Christ principally through the testimony of the apostles and of those prophets who were forerunners of the apostles. The Church is, above all else, apostolic. Whether the Catholic doctrine of apostolic succession is acceptable or not, it must be acknowledged that the apostles are of central importance in the life of the early Church. The solemn opening words of the First Epistle of John, where the "we" clearly refers to the apostolic community, are only one example. "That which was from the beginning, that which we have heard, that which we have seen with our eyes, that which we have beheld, and our hands handled, concerning the Word of Life (and the life was manifested, and we have seen, and bear witness, and declare unto you the life, the eternal life, which was with the Father and was manifested unto us); that which we have seen and heard declare we unto you also, that ye may have fellowship with us; yea, and our fellowship is with the Father, and with His Son, Jesus Christ."

In the same way, although Paul is very anxious in Galatians to make the "Protestant" point that a certain kind of connection with the Jerusalem apostles is unnecessary before his "Gospel" can be accepted, he nevertheless insists that it is to be accepted because he had received an apostolic commission similar to theirs from the risen Lord on the Damascus road. When he is reminding his readers of one of the central truths of the Gospel, he is always at pains to make clear that it is part of the apostolic tradition and that to reject it is equivalent to rejecting Christ. When in such important passages as those recounting the institution of the Lord's Supper in I Corinthians 11:23–25 and the resurrection appearances at the beginning of the fifteenth chapter of the same epistle, he says, "For I received of the Lord that which I delivered unto you," his words have a technical meaning. To receive of the Lord meant to receive, as part of the basic apostolic tradition, the *depositum fidei*, which it was the duty of an apostle to "deliver," to hand over, in such a way that its purity and integrity were fully grasped by the recipients. What was handed over was not a series of interesting and illuminating notes and theories, but the revelatory and saving facts of the faith itself, "the Gospel which ye have received and in which ye stand." It was the truth which was constitutive of the Church, and unless it was handed over and received existentially, the Church was in danger of being built, not on the rock of true faith, but on shifting sand.

It is the fact that they have not always clearly acknowledged the relation between this basic Christian belief and their very existence as churches which weakens the foundations of many of the Liberal Protestant churches today. Whether it is their liberalism as such which is responsible for this is a debatable question. Liberalism is one of the vaguest and most abused of terms. It can refer either to a critical temper of mind which realizes the relativity of all formulations of truth and prompts its adherents to an attitude of humble self-criticism and toler-ance, which is one of the most authentic fruits of the Spirit of Christ, or to a shallow modernism which makes topical rele-vance the criterion of truth.

Protestant churches, especially in English-speaking coun-tries, have had both aspects in recent times, but the latter was particularly strong in the last generation and has had peculiarly damaging consequences for the conception of the Church which has prevailed in those circles where it was influential. For what it did was to try to drive a wedge between Jesus and the apostolic Church. The implication of its position was that the historic Church was founded on a distortion of the teaching of Jesus. Jesus was a wise and attractive teacher, who went about doing good and who gathered around Himself an in-formal group of friends, to whom He expounded His beliefs. Through the perversity and resentment of the exponents of institutional religion, He suffered a noble and inspiring martyr-dom but left his followers with the conviction, mythologized in the resurrection faith, that His influence would live in them if they strove to remember Him and to do what He said. But after His death His followers became so impressed with His idealized memory that they started to invent myths and doc-trines about Him. They made Him a superhuman figure and worker of miracles, and after a time became more concerned with insisting that others agree with their definitions of His nature and work than with fostering the brotherly love which He taught. The "Jesus of history" was lost behind the "Christ of faith," and it was the remote, austere figure of the latter who became the object of devotion in the increasingly elaborate, stylized, and clericalized historic Church.

These ideas, of course, contain a measure of important truth, but do so in such a one-sided and oversimplified way that their influence on the world of scholarship has been brief. Their influence on popular piety and thinking in American and British Protestantism has, however, been very much greater. Books like Fosdick's *Manhood of the Master* and even simpler books like *By an Unknown Disciple,* who was, presumably, held to be more reliable as a witness than those who left us the Gospels, evoked an instant response from large sections of the Protestant public. The result is that the God of many Protestant churches, and of even more Protestant Sunday schools, has been made over into this image of Jesus, which has found acceptable expression in the leading ikon of this cult, Sallman's *Head of Christ.*

The reasons for this are not all discreditable. Jesus does often become a remote and irrelevant figure in the minds of many people and seems to become lost in the rituals of formal ecclesiasticism. It is the temptation of churches to put doctrinal orthodoxy or ritual correctness or legality before love and tolerance. The figure of Jesus of Nazareth, or the Teacher of Galilee, is the same as that of Jesus Christ our Saviour, and it is right that it should be given its full significance. But a faith based on Jesus of Nazareth alone, and a very carefully edited picture of Him at that, ignores the most important things about Him, evades life's deepest questions, and misleads the Church as to its true nature.

To begin with, examination of the New Testament proves that the attempt to make a sharp distinction between the Jesus of history and the Christ of faith breaks down. The earliest and most primitive Gospel, Mark, opens with the words, "The beginning of the gospel of Jesus Christ, the Son of God," and is

written to demonstrate the lordship of Christ. It says nothing
about the birth, boyhood, and young manhood of Jesus, does
not devote a great deal of attention to the Galilean ministry,
and concentrates its chief attention on His sufferings and death.
The early sermons in Acts and most of the Pauline epistles
were probably written earlier than Mark, and they proclaim
the Christ of the Church's faith. To make Paul the villain of
the piece is quite unjustifiable. Recent scholarship has shown
that there is much more unity to be found between the different
parts of the New Testament than was visible in the first flush of
enthusiasm for source criticism, and the Pauline faith is not
substantially different from that of the Gospels. Is it likely that,
from the beginning, the Church was radically mistaken in its
conception of the nature and teaching of Jesus, and that it was
only in the late nineteenth century that the outlines of a true
picture were discovered, especially when the picture so discovered bears a remarkable likeness to the ideal figure of a good
man current at that time?

The consequences of this attempt to base faith on a semi-
fictitious picture of Jesus were particularly grave for the efforts
at self-understanding of the churches to which people who held
these views belonged. For the Church is founded not only on
certain facts about the ministry of Jesus but also on a conviction
that God has honored in the past and continues still to honor
the interpretation put upon these facts by the Spirit-led community of Christ's people. The event and its interpretation are
inextricably fused together in the Bible. This is as true of Mark
as it is of John. Critical scholarship has the duty of trying to
isolate the historical event from the Church's interpretation of
it, but that is not the same as taking it for granted that the interpretation is necessarily false.

The apostolic witness to Christ is made "from faith to faith."
That does not mean that it must be received with an attitude of

unintelligent credulity or without a recognition that it can be substantially true and yet erroneous in detail, but it does mean that its recipient must respect the integrity of the writers of Scripture. He knows that the God who spoke to them has spoken to him also. To take it for granted that they are unreliable means that "they are found false witnesses of Christ" and that the Church they founded was based on misconceptions. It is hard to conceive of a breach of fellowship within the body of the Church which could be more radical than that.

It is only in a few churches, generally of a Unitarian type, that this attitude has become as explicit as that, but its diffused influence in popular Protestantism has been great. The result has been that these churches have been embarrassed in relation to the Bible and the Creeds and the witness to the Christian faith of the Church throughout the ages. They have taken refuge in a truncated version of Christianity, which has been trimmed to their own preconceptions, and they have lost their grip on that dimension of experience where they are at one with Abraham and Moses and the prophets and the apostles and the whole family of God throughout the ages. They have lost tradition, in the sense of the living stream of the whole Church's life flowing down from the past to enrich the present, and in consequence they have had difficulty in distinguishing the Spirit of the living God from the spirit of the age. They have become more and more like clubs for those of similar background and social circumstances who are united in believing that a little religion is a "good thing" and in indulging in experiments within the religious dimension, without much sense of responsibility to what other Christians believe to be the revealed will of God.

If the danger to which modern Liberal Protestantism has been exposed has been that of denying the apostolic foundation of the Church, Catholicism is exposed to the danger of so defining the nature of that apostolic foundation as to distort its nature. Granting that the Church must stand in the succession of the apostles if it is to be true to its origin, in what does that succession consist? It is here that sharp division arises between Christian groups. Those Protestants who would claim that their position is congruous with the Church of the New Testament insist that what constitutes the claim of the apostles upon men of the present day is not any power they possessed which is automatically transferable to others who could then pass it on as automatically to those who came after them. It is the fact that they were chosen and empowered by Christ to be His witnesses. It is, therefore, their testimony to Christ which constitutes their claim upon the Church of the present day. If men wish to stand in their succession, it is less important that they belong to the right kind of institution and that they should have received the right kind of certification than that they should heed and act upon that testimony. Those stand in the succession of the apostles who seek to be obedient to Christ.

It is true that this is likely to involve loyalty to those institutional forms of the Church which strive to express that obedience, but such loyalty of itself provides no sufficient guarantee that that obedience will be fulfilled. One of the most striking reminders of the truth of this is given right at the beginning of the story of the Church of the New Covenant. When the disciples are casting their nets at the Sea of Tiberias without the presence and direction of their risen Lord, they can do nothing. All night they cast their nets in vain. But when they do so at His command, even though they are unable adequately to recognize Him, their net is filled with one hundred fifty-three fishes, the number which represents a perfect catch.

Where this is not freely acknowledged, the Church is in danger of living by some self-generating worldly power of

her own rather than by the Spirit of Christ. If Protestant
churches sometimes give the impression of living by their inherent vitality as successful community institutions, Catholic
churches equally give the impression of living by the "spirit of
Catholicism" rather than by the power of the living Christ. The
only way truly to stand in the succession of the apostles is by
striving to share their faith and to fulfill a similar personal
responsibility to Christ in the Spirit. This is a task which confronts not only ministers, although they have special obligations in this matter, but the whole membership of a church.
They must strive to "continue steadfastly in the apostles' teaching, in the breaking of bread and the prayers." If it be asked
how a church can be sure that it is doing this, the answer is
clear and well enough known. It is that it possesses the Holy
Scriptures and must try to be faithful to their teaching. These
are the records deliberately left by the apostolic community
by which they strove to ensure that, after they had passed
away, there should be no doubt as to what their authentic
teaching was. They are supported by the testimony of primitive
liturgies and other records, but the Scriptures stand supreme.
It is for this reason that Protestants insist so firmly on the
authority of Scripture as against that of the teaching Church,
of which Catholicism makes so much.

This is not, however, merely to set the authority of a book
against that of a living tradition, any more than it is to confer
a static infallibility on every word of the book. For the apostles
would have regarded their testimony as misleading unless it
led men to an existential encounter with Jesus Christ and they
would have insisted that He was misunderstood, as the Jews
misunderstood Him, unless He transformed their lives. It is this
living knowledge of Jesus Christ which constitutes the Church
as the Church and which enables a modern church to stand in
the succession of the apostles. This is what lies behind the clas-

sic Reformed definition of the Church as the body in which the
Word is faithfully preached, the sacraments are administered
according to Christ's ordinance, and a zealous and disciplined
effort is made to practice the Christian life. That may sound a
very austere definition of the Church in the ears of many members of the Reformed churches themselves, but it goes to the
heart of the matter because it makes clear that it is the attempt
to know Christ through His appointed means and to follow Him
which constitutes the reality of the Church.

An important implication of this is that the possibility of
straying from Christ is always open to any part of the Church.
If the Church is to remain faithful to Christ, it must always be
turning back to Christ as the Bible declares Him and reforming
its life in the light of His truth. The rhythm of its life is one of
particular acts of repentance, reformation, and renewal. Where
this is broken, the Church becomes conformed to this "world
which passeth away" and ceases to live by the power of Christ.
This, as we shall see, determines the way in which the Church
should organize its worship and its common life. It is this which
is the purpose of church order.

CHAPTER VII

The Purpose of Church Order

The term "church order" has a specific connotation for the theologian. It means more than church organization or even church government. It refers to the shape which the Church has in the world as it strives to be conformed to the will of Christ who is its Head. Christian believers have a duty to gather together into church order. They must behave in the Spirit of Christ to all men, whether they call themselves Christian or not, but with those who share their Christian belief they are able to live together in unity as members of the family of God. In obedience to Christ, they have the responsibility for ensuring that the life and work of His people are carried forward in the world. They must make arrangements for the adequate preaching of the Word and for the administration of the sacraments by a gifted and learned ministry. They must live together in a fellowship richer than that which is possible with those who do not acknowledge the name of Christ. They must seek to discover Christ's will for His people in the ever-changing circumstances of life. They must engage in evangelism, mutual care, and the works of reconciliation and compassion which are the responsibility and privilege of the people of God.

This language is more appropriate to Protestantism than to Catholicism, and it reflects important differences of emphasis, but it is worth observing that the differences between the two forms of churchmanship are not quite as great here as they might appear to be. Most forms of Protestantism, at least, would agree with Catholicism that the Church must have a definite shape in the world and that that shape is controlled by the nature of the work which the Church has to do. Catholics may call it "the structure of Catholicism"[1] or "the form of the Church,"[2] and Protestants may prefer to call it "church order," or, to use a phrase of John Owen, the Independent divine of the seventeenth century, "the ordinance of Christ for His Church," but it is the same reality of which both speak.

A Christian community responsibly gathered into church order would seem to require the faithful proclamation of the Word, the regular administration of the Gospel sacraments, a ministry sufficiently learned and gifted to perform these offices adequately, an organ of church government which expresses the responsibility of the whole body to see that the proper work of the Church is performed, in worship, evangelism, oversight, education, mutual care and service, and a means of effective communion between the particular church and wider fellowship of churches. Most churches would add that the faithful proclamation of the Word involves a recognition of the authority of the Bible and some form of declaration on the Church's part of its determination to continue in the apostles' teaching, whether through acceptance of the Ecumenical Creeds or through an official confessional statement.

Before we proceed to the detailed discussion of these parts

[1] As in *The Gospel and the Catholic Church*, by A. M. Ramsey (Longmans, London, 1937).
[2] As in *The Form of the Church*, by A. G. Hebert (Faber, London, 1944).

of church order, three points of a general character should be
borne in mind. First, while history and present experience
seem to show that an order of this kind is necessary for the
effective functioning of the Church, it is important that it
should not be too rigidly conceived and that Christ should not
be irrevocably tied to such a form. To imagine such things is
to run into what we have already seen to be the characteristic
ecclesiastical danger, that of subordinating Christ to the
Church. It would be to idolize the secondary forms of the
Church rather than the Christ to whom they point, and therefore to challenge Christ's claim to be master in His own house.
As T.F. Torrance has put it in a difficult but very important sentence, "Surely the essential form of the visible Church wherein
she images her Lord is to be found in her humble service in
which the great reconciliation already wrought out in the Body
of Christ is lived out among men, and the Church in life and
action becomes, as it were, sacramentally correlative to the life
and passion of Jesus Christ?"[3] Even in its handling of the means
of grace entrusted to its care, the Church must never forget
that it exists in the form of a servant and that the divine initiative is not given over completely into its hands.

The importance of this is underlined by the fact, for which
there is abundant evidence, that churches which have con-
siderably less than full church order by Catholic or well-
established Protestant standards are able to bring forth fruits of
the Spirit. The Society of Friends and the Salvation Army
lack the sacraments. Many churches, especially in Catholic
lands, lack true evangelical preaching. In many others, especially in the Orthodox East and in some Roman Catholic
countries, the Bible can hardly be said to be a significantly
open book, and they appear to subsist by the Gospel in the

[3]From "Concerning Amsterdam" in the *Scottish Journal of Theology,*
1949.

Liturgy. Even more churches lack organs through which the laity can effectively express their responsibility for the work of the Church. Yet a little leaven leaveneth the whole lump, in the internal life of the Church as it does in the Church's relation to the world. As long as Christ finds some entry into the life of churches, He is able to make His Word prosper and multiply. To the extent that churches lack some elements of what we believe to be the true order, their life is impoverished, but it is not anyone's business to deny the Christian name to them if they claim it for themselves and show something of the humility and teachability of true followers of Christ. God knows His own better than do any of His children, and His children should have the grace to accept that fact.

This is a point which clerics in the various denominations would do particularly well to bear in mind. Christ's body stands out as a whole clearly enough against the background of the rest of mankind, but all its parts are not equally defined and it is sometimes hard to say exactly where the Church ends and the world begins. This may make life extremely difficult for church administrators, but they can make things easier for themselves only by unchurching those whom Christ has clearly chosen to bless.

Thirdly, church order must never be thought of in too static a fashion. It is a clerical temptation to think of the Church only as an organism, and preferably a vegetable rather than as an animal. But in this conflict the metaphor of an army on the march is much better. The purpose of church order is to ensure that the people of God are kept moving toward their true destination rather than to perfect the organization and to define the limits of the temporary camps of their earthly pilgrimage. We seek a country which is not here, and the element of the provisional and the makeshift is inescapably present in the Church's form in this world. Those Christians who break out

into new territory and in so doing fall foul of existing Church
organizations are not wrong in protesting that many churches
appear to regard church order as a means of keeping the
Spirit safely domesticated within man-made bounds. Too
many churches are rigid and muscle-bound, and use nearly all
their limited energies in justifying their immobility. Church
order, in worship, ministry, and organization, is misconceived
if it is not seen as the primary means for preventing the people
of God from striking roots in this passing world, from being, in
the precise sense of that word, secularized.

It is this insight which partly lies behind the fashionable
modern insistence on speaking of the Church in eschatological
terms. The order of the Church must not be conformed to this
world which passeth away but to that which is to come. God's
Spirit leads His people as a pillar of cloud by day and of fire
by night out of the Egypt of their sins to the Promised Land
which is their eternal home. It is not a capricious Spirit, but the
Spirit of the Lord Jesus Christ who has revealed the Father.
But it is a Spirit which never gives itself over into our possession. It is always before men, beckoning them forward, and
church order fulfills its true purpose only if it enables them to
discern and follow that Spirit's guidance.

CHAPTER VIII

The Word of God and the Church

Primacy is given to the Word and sacraments in defining the marks of the Church because they express the Church's concrete recognition that it is God in Jesus Christ who is the source of its life. The proclamation of God's Word is a means of grace, one of the essential ways in which Jesus Christ makes Himself known and imparts His divine life to men. The Church is called to preach the Gospel, to declare the Good News of God, to all people, and when she does so, the promise is that the Holy Spirit will enable her to speak the living Word of Christ, which carries His own redemptive power.

First, the term "the Word" must be defined. It is very freely used in these days, often in ways which serve to confuse as much as they enlighten. Its fundamental meaning, of course, is God's speech to man, what God says when He addresses man. This is the "word of the Lord" which came to the prophet. It is summed up in Jesus Christ, God's decisive Word. He is God's Word, not merely to men but to Himself, the eternal Word, through whom the worlds were framed.

It is not arbitrary to speak of Jesus Christ as the Word of

God in this way. The Prologue to the Fourth Gospel and the
first chapter of the Epistle to the Hebrews both do it. It can be
seen, also, that this is the most fitting title for Jesus Christ. For
speech is the most personal, the most characteristically human,
and also the most fully articulated and precise mode of com-
munication. He speaks in deeds as well as in words, but, in the
Hebrew mind, word and deed were inseparably connected.
The interpretation was part of the event. To call Jesus Christ
the Word of God is the most emphatic way of asserting the
rationality of divine revelation, God's determination to make
sense to man on the most responsible and verifiable level of experience.

This Word of God in Jesus Christ is given to us in human
words, recorded in the way human words are, in writing, in the
Scriptures. It has become the custom, therefore, to speak of the
Bible also as the Word of God. It is doubtful whether this is a
correct use of language, and it has led to an idolatry of the
letter of the Bible which is on a level with that idolatry of the
forms of the Church which was mentioned in the last section.
The Bible is not infallible, and the words which it records and
the way in which it records them have their share of the im-
perfection and contingency which affect even the most precise forms of language. To discern the living Word in the
written Word requires training and Spirit-guided insight. Yet
the fact remains that it is through these words, as through no
other medium, that God's Word in Jesus Christ is heard.

But the matter does not rest there. Just because God's Word
is living, it does not remain incarcerated within the pages of
Scripture or in the past history of the Church. Jesus Christ in
the Spirit speaks to His people now. He speaks out of the
Scriptures and in a way congruous with what He has said in the
past, but He speaks a new word which is directly addressed to
their present condition. The Spirit fulfills the promise of John

16:13, not in the sense of making the Church recall the *ipsissima verba* of Jesus' utterances on earth but in the sense of enabling the teaching Christ to be present anew in the Church's midst, speaking no longer in parables but in clear guidance for present tasks.

It is this waiting upon the living Christ in the Spirit which is the primary means of grace in the Church, for through it the Church hears the Word by which it lives. This is an activity of much wider scope than that of the sermon of the minister, but it receives its clearest expression in the sermon, and a discussion of the sermon will best reveal its nature.

Many churches do not give a great deal of prominence to the sermon in worship. This makes them defective as churches, although, in some instances, they contrive to hear the Word of God in other forms. But even in those Protestant churches where the sermon is exalted, considerable confusion as to its precise function exists among ministers no less than among their people. This is a weakness which eats at the heart of the Church's life. The sermon is radically misunderstood if it is thought of as a discourse about life in general proffered by someone who imagines that his chief title to speak consists in his knowledge, eloquence, personal magnetism, or good nature, and who hopes that his observations, which may well be based on some striking instance of the human situation which occurs in the Bible, will serve to enlighten, encourage, comfort, and possibly even inspire his hearers in their attitude toward life. It is also not much more fully understood if it is taken to be, as it is in many Catholic churches, a form of instruction, an articulation of the mind of the Church, already given in tradition and applied to a particular situation by a duly authorized teacher, who may add to it a note of exhortation and emotional appeal. The sermon stands by itself as a distinctive activity, and its nature is determined by the relation between God's revelation in Christ and the Church.

Preaching starts from that revelation as it is given in Scripture. It is that which gives the preacher his authority and determines the way in which he should fulfill his task. Scripture, however, is not the private possession of the minister or of a special ministerial caste. It is in the hands of the people, and they have direct access to what it says. The people are not dependent on the ministry, therefore, for any knowledge they may possess of Christ. Yet an act of ministry is essential if, as a Church, they are to hear the Word of Christ and discover His will for their common life.

Consider what is involved in an act of true preaching. First, a revelatory word or deed of God has to be studied carefully in its own situation if its meaning for those to whom it originally came is to be understood aright. This involves some knowledge of biblical studies, in all their complexity. Secondly, it needs to be looked at also in the light of the whole movement of God's self-revelation in Scripture and of the Church's experience of the ways of God throughout the ages. This involves a knowledge of biblical theology and church history. Thirdly, it has to be related to the present condition of the worshiping group, both as this is known in its distinctiveness through the minister's intimate pastoral dealings with it and as it is seen in the setting of the whole life of the Church in the world of the present day. This involves the ability to think theologically in relation to the conditions of modern thought and life. Without this equipment, the ability of the Church to hear what Christ is saying to it is gravely impaired.

This is not meant to imply that the individual believer is incapable of reading and understanding the Bible for himself. On the contrary, it assumes that he is doing so. A good congregation nearly always has its Bibles open before it during the preaching, and one important function of the preacher is so to teach and guide the people that they are able to read their Bibles on their own with more intelligence and critical discrimination. But there are at least three reasons which make something like the public ministry of preaching an essential part of the Church's life.

First, there is the obvious practical consideration. It may be theoretically possible for the ordinary member of the congregation to discover all that is necessary for adequate reading of Scripture for himself, but it is unlikely that he will, especially to the level of accurate scholarship and professional efficiency which is desirable in dealing with such important matters. When the amount of specialism which modern life demands is borne in mind, it becomes hardly necessary to apologize for a measure of specialism in this grave and complicated realm.

Secondly, the history of the Church seems to show that a calling from God and the possession of certain spiritual gifts are both requisite and forthcoming for the adequate fulfillment of this office. Whatever view we may hold of the form which the apostolic succession takes in the Church, we may agree that God raises up a succession of apostolic men to continue the apostolic work of preaching. To define preaching, in Phillips Brooks' oft-quoted phrase, as "truth through personality" is most inadequate and misleading, yet preaching does seem to require a gift which is not bestowed upon every man. A certain intensity of spiritual apprehension and a willingness to face issues which other men are often happy to avoid, qualities which carry their own distinctive temptations with them, seem to be necessary, and they do not readily come except to those upon whom God lays hold as He did upon the prophets of Israel. Spiritual gifts are to be distinguished from those of intellect or even of imagination. These are obviously desirable, but without the gift of spiritual apprehension they are of no avail.

At the same time, essential as this gift is, it is not the only qualification for a minister. This is the mistake often made by spiritual enthusiasts, especially if they belong to new sects. The minister needs to be learned in the sense described above, as well as gifted, if he is to fulfill his ministry. The possession of a spiritual gift is an indication that a man is suitable for training for the ministry, but it is only in very exceptional cases that it can be a substitute for this training, and anyone who uses his alleged possession of it as an excuse for not undergoing training raises the suspicion that he "hath a demon" rather than the Spirit of Christ.

Thirdly, the preaching of the Word is a public act. It is addressed not only to the individual but to the Church as a body, and through the Church to the world on which Christ sets His claim. It is a corrupt form of individualism which assumes that the most important and the most genuine part of the Christian life is private. God's dealings are with His people, and with individuals as members of the body of Christ. Public reading and preaching of the Word are the essential complement of its private study, without which private study can go selfishly astray. The Word is misheard if it is not heard in the context of the family life of the people of God and of His eternal purpose for mankind.

It will be clear from this that the greatest sin of the faithful minister is to thrust his own personality between the people and the Word of God. He is commissioned by the Church to lead it in hearing the Word of God, in "opening" the world of the Bible so that all may enter it. He himself can be a living witness to the power of Christ, but it is not his chief function in the preaching to strive to make himself one. His task is the more modest and practicable one, which will yet require all the gifts and graces with which God has endowed him, of being the servant of the Church's service. He must, of course, be personally involved in what he says and does. Preaching is the nearest to "existential thinking" of any form of discourse. But that does not entitle him to inflict his private preoccupations upon his congregation. It is not himself but Christ whom he ministers, and Christ cannot be ministered except by one who is in the form of a servant. The servant is not greater than his Lord, neither he that is sent greater than he that sent him. The minister's words must always be conformed to the mind of Christ. If he contrives to make people concentrate on him, even in admiration, rather than on God in Christ, he is failing as a minister. Part of the reason why ministers study theology in a systematic and critical way is to equip themselves to check what they preach by God's self-revelation, so that they can be on their guard against preaching words of their own in place of the Word of God. Theology can be defined as the intellectual side of the minister's personal self-examination, leading to constant repentance and reformation in relation to his central ministerial activity.

To see preaching in this light should give both ministers and people a feeling of release. It makes preaching a feasible activity for weak and sinful men. In virtually denying that preaching was the ministry of the Word of God, Liberal Protestantism condemned its ministers to shouldering the intolerable burden of trying to feed the people out of their own miserable store of wisdom and insight and sense of life. There is no more invidious position for a man than to have to occupy twenty-five minutes or so of the attention of his fellows in such a way as to conceal from them the fact that the Word of God is absent. It is no wonder that so many have given up under the strain and taken refuge in anecdotal and repetitive triviality.

The other side of this is that no men are more deserving of the sympathetic co-operation of their fellows than those who genuinely try to help them listen to what God is saying to them,

carefully spelling out the precise meaning of Scripture, strug-
gling to ascertain its guidance for their particular situation,
vigilantly guarding against possible misunderstanding, anxious
to follow any light which the Christian experience of others
may have to give. When the early Puritans wished to speak
with approval of a minister, they called him a "painful
preacher of the Word." That meant that he took the utmost
pains to ensure that it was God's own Word that he was preaching and that it genuinely went home in the lives of those to
whom he ministered.

Even if a man is a painful preacher in the sense which more
naturally suggests itself to modern minds, lacking eloquence
and fire and imaginative power, he has a claim on the humble
and patient attention of his hearers if he genuinely strives to
open the Scriptures for them. He is, at least, trying to make the
sermon an instrument with which they can wait together upon
God. But even if he is the most silvery-tongued and dynamic of
spellbinders, with all the statistics from *Time* magazine and
the little stories from the *Reader's Digest* ready to hand, it is
an impertinent imposition for him to thrust his irrelevant clev-
erness upon a congregation who should be seeking guidance
from God in His Word. The saving virtue of true preaching is
not eloquence or sincerity: it is faithfulness.

The implication of this is that preaching must be thought of
as much more of a corporate activity than it is often taken to
be. The congregation is not an audience. It is a legitimate
Catholic criticism of Protestant churches that many of them
have been built on that assumption, and in more fundamental
ways than architecturally. Protestant congregations, especially
of the freer sort, are quick to insist that their ministers do not
form a separate caste but are members of the church with a
special function to perform. If that is true of the person of the
minister, it is no less true of his function of preaching sermons.

The sermon is an activity of the congregation, and it should be listened to responsibly, with a realization that it is meant to make a difference to their life together and should not go either unheeded or, if need be, unchallenged. This does not make the minister the mere hireling or toady of the congregation. He is the minister to them, not of their own pet ideas, but of the Word of God, and he has a right to insist that if they challenge what he says they do so by appeal to the authority of the Word of God which both recognize, if necessary as interpreted by representatives of the wider life of the Church. Some congregations have such a false conception of their relation to their minister that his freedom to preach God's Word along the whole range of life must be safeguarded, but that does not affect the fact that the link between preaching and the Church's common life needs to be re-emphasized in these days.

Preaching is not merely a matter of trying to induce generalized decisions for Jesus Christ on the part of particular individuals. It is also a matter of helping the Church to reach specific decisions about its life as part of the people of God. It is also more than an invocation of the memory of an absent Lord or the recapitulation of the broad outlines of the meaning of His work. It is the realization of the presence in the midst of the living Christ, whose Word is still mighty to the casting down of strongholds and who is still able to bring every thought of His wayward disciples into His captivity.

Something is meant to happen in preaching, and results should be expected from it. Those Christian bodies who make a feature of encouraging such expectancy tend to do so too much in terms of the production of stereotyped forms of individual conversion experience, but the fact that their expectancy is so limited and one-sided should not lead others to assume that the results of preaching must always be so indirect as to be indiscernible. The Christian life is not primarily a matter either of

constantly renewed experiences of conversion or of vaguely
edifying spirituality. It is a matter of concrete day-to-day
acts of obedience made both by individuals and the Christian
community, and preaching should be directed toward guiding
and confirming people in the way of that obedience.

Does this mean that preaching must always take place
within the congregation and be directed only to those who are
committed Christians? It is true that a great deal of preaching
should be pastoral in character and internal to the life of the
Church. From some points of view, the minister is the "back-
room boy" or the resource person in the life of the Church, and
the most effective impact on the rest of the community is made
by the general membership of the Church whom he exists to
serve. It is certainly erroneous to think of him chiefly as the
Church's public relations officer. At the same time, the Church
has a responsibility to proclaim the Word of God directly to all
who will hear it, "that all might be saved and come to the
knowledge of the truth." The minister will take his full share
in this and will always remind his congregation of their wider
responsibilities to mankind. More than that, he will not forget
that all men, whether they are professing Christians or not, are
open to the temptations of unbelief. The human situation is not
fundamentally different from one person to another. He will be
a bad preacher if he does not constantly have to grapple with
unbelief, and he will not need to go outside the Church, or outside his own heart, in order to find it. Many passages of Scripture are unintelligible unless he does this, because faith always
vindicates itself in terms of a conflict with its opposite. To
speak to the real condition of his own people will often be the
most effective way of speaking to those who are outside. This
does not rule out his speaking to those outside in other ways
than by inducing them to attend the assemblies of the Church.
The Church has become too stereotyped in this way also, and

there is a clear need today for a more informal and flexible proclamation of the Gospel, especially through personal conversation. The fact that it will have to observe the modest conventions of conversation, with its give-and-take, instead of the more self-important conventions of oratory, will not necessarily make it any the less truly a proclamation of the Word.

Rigidity must also be guarded against in answering the question of whether all preaching must be the exposition of a single text of Scripture. The expository sermon should certainly be the norm, and those who depart from it very frequently should ask themselves honestly whether they are being faithful to their vocation. This in itself, of course, is not to say that the verse is the only appropriate portion of Scripture to be expounded. A lengthy passage, a parable, a prophecy, a whole book, the life of an individual or, at the other extreme, a single word like "agape" or "koinonia," all constitute legitimate texts. But in these days, when people have often ceased to be familiar with the Bible and their jaded appetites are unable to endure a full diet of the Word, they must often be approached by indirect means. It is not wrong to start from some topic of current interest and discover what light the mind of Christ throws upon it, or to lead people to the Bible rather than to lead them from the Bible to their own situation. Pastoral wisdom is an essential element in faithful preaching and it must be given freedom of action. But it should not be made an excuse, as it often has been, for evading the full magnitude of the task of proclaiming Christ as the Scriptures declare Him. The trivialization of preaching is one of the chief sources of weakness in the Church. The Church lives only by the Word of God, and the minister betrays his own unbelief and becomes a blind leader of the blind if he does not bend all his energies toward helping the Church hear that Word for itself as the true and living Word which is the source of its own life.

CHAPTER IX

The Sacraments

The sacraments, and in particular the Lord's Supper or Eucharist or Mass, as it is variously called, are the primary means of grace to many Christians. To most Catholics the ideas expressed in the last chapter will seem strange, for they hold their communion with Christ in the sacrament of His body and blood. On the other hand, the most characteristic attitude of non-Anglican and non-Lutheran Protestants toward the sacraments in these days is one of embarrassment. The only notable exceptions are fervent Baptists over the specific matter of "believers' baptism." The uncompromising assertion of both the Gospel sacraments on the prevenient grace of God troubles the religious subjectivism of popular Protestantism, and their frank use of material elements—bread, wine, and water—troubles their spiritual-mindedness. Modern Protestantism has inclined, therefore, to oscillate between an aesthetic symbolism, which sees the sacraments primarily as a beautiful pageant, and a common-sense attitude which sees baptism as a form of dedication to Christian service and the Lord's Supper as a fellowship meal where inspiration is received from the memory of Christ's sacrificial love and resolutions are made to follow Him more closely.

According to the classical teaching of most Protestant churches, however, the sacraments should have a much more central place in the life of the Church than that. Baptism and the Lord's Supper are part of the means of grace. They are ways by which men know Christ and receive His benefits. What is true of the Word is true of them also, in another form. It has been said that in the preaching the emphasis is on the *Word* made flesh; but that in the sacraments, chiefly the Lord's Supper, it is on the Word made *flesh*. Whether that is the most appropriate way of putting it or not, it reminds us that Word and sacraments go together and belong to the same order of reality.

Why are sacraments necessary? Could not the faith of the Church subsist perfectly well without these oriental rites, which presuppose a way of thinking and acting which is very different from that which comes naturally to people who live in the modern Western world? It must be admitted that faith can undoubtedly exist without sacraments, because churches which bring forth a measure of the fruit of the Spirit exist without them. Yet this fact is hard to contest: that the chief reason why Christians have sacraments is because their Lord instituted them. They are a gift of Christ, to be used in His service, and His followers have no right to decline the gift. The dominical institution of Baptism is not so clear-cut as that of the Lord's Supper, but the fact that from the beginning the Church baptized in the name of Christ makes a strong prima-facie case in its favor. There is a certain giveness about the sacraments which has to be recognized and which it is a proper exercise of humble Christian obedience to accept. "Go ye and baptize." "This do in remembrance of me." It is theoretically possible to envisage the use of elements other than water and bread and wine, and rites other than washing and breaking and pouring out, but the fact is that it is these which were appointed and the Church must respect the wisdom of its Lord.

Nevertheless, it would be difficult to accept this institution of Christ if there were any strong reason to suppose that His appointment was merely arbitrary or capricious. The fact that the sacraments have been cherished so widely throughout Christendom and Christian history, even to the point of excess and distortion in some traditions, indicates that they effectively fulfill Christ's promise. To quote some famous words of Calvin, "A sacrament is an outward sign wherewith the Lord sealeth to our consciences the promises of His good will toward us, to sustain the weakness of our faith; and we again, on our behalf, do testify our godliness toward Him as well before Him and the angels as before men" (*Institutio* 4,14,1). The mode of expression is archaic, but the ideas are of permanent validity. They remind us that sacraments are but the outward signs of a reality which is apprehended in faith. They are not themselves that reality. Calvin insists, in contrast to Roman Catholic teaching, that the water remains water and that the substance of the bread and wine is not changed. They are seals attaching to the promise of God in Christ, and without the promise they are as meaningless as a seal attached to a parchment which has nothing written upon it.

It is not the faith of the recipients which is the source of the reality of the sacraments, but the promise, the fact that God has spoken His Word of forgiveness and newness of life in Christ. Nevertheless, this does not mean that faith is unnecessary. When the sacramental elements are not received in faith, God is dishonored and His graciousness and hospitality are made light of, but the sin consists in denying God, not in receiving the corporeal presence of Jesus Christ into our bodies in contempt of Him. It may seem that this is a distinction without a difference, but that is not quite true. For to put it in this way means that the chief emphasis remains on the primacy of the divine action and the worship of the people is fixed, not on the physical elements, but on Christ the Redeemer and the Host.

This, in its turn, is not to suggest that the rites themselves are unimportant. Christ promised and has vindicated His promise that He will meet with His people specifically through these forms. To think of them as memorials is not enough. The overwhelming testimony of Christian experience throughout the ages is that He is present in the midst during the sacraments, speaking His personal word as He does in the preaching. If He is not, then those who say that sacraments are no more than edifying rituals, in which only those who have a temperamental inclination toward them need participate, are right. But this real presence of Christ can be insisted upon without claiming that He is localized in the elements. The essence of the sacraments lies in the sacramental action. As Nathaniel Micklem has put it, "The efficacy of Baptism is not in water but in washing, of the Communion not in bread but in bread broken. The elements are as integral to the sacrament as the words to the sentence, but as it is the whole sentence alone which is effectual as conveying meaning, so it is the Word (and not the elements) that convey grace in the Sacrament."[1]

That this characteristic insight of the Reformation is faithful to the mind of the early Church has been shown by the researches of an Anglo-Catholic scholar who had no predisposition to favor the Reformers, the late Dom Gregory Dix. In his book *The Shape of the Liturgy* he pointed out that it was the custom of the early Church to think not of saying or offering the Eucharist but of doing it. To illustrate from the Lord's Supper, the grace is given through the whole action, which in-

[1] In *Christian Worship* (Oxford, 1936), p. 245.

cludes meeting together before the Lord's Table, hearing His word of forgiveness and promise, going forward to receive the bread and wine, broken and poured out according to His institution. The fact that Catholicism can see the truth of the fact that the essence of the sacraments consists in the action rather than in the species more clearly in regard to baptism than to the Lord's Supper suggests that Catholic thought is out of focus at this important point.

In view of the fact that churches are more divided over the sacraments, which above all things should express their unity, than over any other matters, it should be underlined that the differences between them are not necessarily so insurmountable as might at first appear. It is true that Protestants disagree with Catholics as to the way in which the Real Presence of Christ is found in the Lord's Supper, denying that His body is present as the transformed substance lying behind the accidents of bread and wine. But even the most memorialist Protestant would not deny that Christ was present in the midst at the Communion, as the Lord of the feast dispensing His grace to His people through actions undertaken by them in conformity with the nature of that grace.

The sacraments do not stand by themselves in the Church's life any more than the sacramental elements stand alone in the service. They receive their full significance only in the setting of the general life of the Church. It has frequently been pointed out that it was the original intention of the Protestant Reformers that sermon and sacrament should be linked together as the normal Lord's Day service, and that they failed to establish this as the practice because the people, who had been accustomed to communicate only very rarely in the unreformed Church, could not be prevailed upon to come to the Lord's Table more frequently.

It has not been seen so often that the sacrament should also flow out into the general life of the Church. The words of the minister at the Lord's Table, "The peace of the Lord Jesus Christ go with you all" or "Go in peace," are a commission to the members of the Church to carry out into their dealings with their neighbors the reconciliation between God and themselves and each other which has been re-established in the sacrament. And although Protestants disagree with Catholics in regarding penance, confirmation, matrimony, extreme unction, and chrism as sacraments, because they do not believe they are of dominical institution, these practices have the merit of underlining the truth that all parts of the Church's life should be sacramental. It is only when sacraments are seen as an integral part of the Church's life, neither all-important nor unimportant, that they can be delivered from the twin dangers of superstition and trivialization which beset them and are made to fulfill their true function of building up the whole body of Christ in His love.

CHAPTER X

Baptism

"Baptism," says Calvin, "is a sign of the entering wherewith we are received into fellowship of the Church, that, being grafted into Christ, we may be reckoned among the children of God." It is the sacrament of the new birth which His people know in Christ, the sign of their entry into membership of Israel. It is the door into the Church, symbolized in many churches by the placing of the font at the entrance of the building. It marks the end of the journey to Christ and the beginning of the journey in Christ.

The Christian faith does not teach that men are saved by baptism alone. They are saved by Christ, the Word of God, embraced in faith. Baptism provides no automatic regeneration. Protestants criticize Catholic teaching for implying that it does, but it is doubtful whether responsible Catholic teaching would ever put it as simply as that. It is not the water used in baptism which is the cleansing power but the sacrificial life of Jesus Christ which the water symbolizes. Once again, this is not to say that the rite is but an insignificant piece of symbolism. Baptism is a mode of the Word, a way in which God declares His purpose of grace to men. It is this, not because of any magical power inherent in the water, but because it declares and seals the Word. As Nathaniel Micklem has put it, "The prodigal in the far country may receive a message that his father will forgive him or has forgiven him. On his return it is his father's kiss which ratifies and seals the promise, nor would it occur to the prodigal to deny that the kiss is a vehicle of grace. In the gospel the message of washing and sanctifying is brought to us; the message is sealed in baptism."[1]

The meaning of baptism is that Christ, acting through His body, the Church, assures the believer that his sins are forgiven and that he can live as a child of God by the power of God forever, and that He seals this engagement in an act which expresses the cleansing which He wrought for men by His cross and the newness of life into which they rise by His resurrection. In the Bible, baptism is closely linked with the Holy Spirit. The baptized live by the Spirit, as God's free men, the children of the light and of the day, conformed to that new age which will come in its fullness when Christ gathers all things to Himself.

Three considerations need to be borne in mind in relation to baptism in these days. First, baptism has little meaning apart from faith in the redeeming work of Christ. Nowhere is the nature of the Gospel declared more uncompromisingly than here. Believers are buried with Christ and also rise with Him. They acknowledge themselves sinners who can be made clean only by the blood of Christ and rejoice in His power to do so. It is ironical that this service of all services should be the one in which merely formal adherents of the Church most frequently participate. Their embarrassment at the service is easily explicable. It is embarrassment at the declaration of the apostolic Gospel in its starkest form.

[1] In *Christian Worship* (Oxford, 1936).

Secondly, baptism is primarily an act of the Church, not of an individual or of a natural family. It is the act in which believers, and those whom God has given them, are received into the fellowship of the Church. It is not a private transaction between Christ and the individual or a domestic occasion of the family, but a public event, in which the Church celebrates the victorious power of the risen and ascended Christ over sin, death, and the devil, ratified anew in the instance of another member of the people of God. That is why baptism should not be treated simply as an optional extra in the life of the believer and why private baptisms are so undesirable. The assembly of the Church for public worship on the Lord's Day is the most suitable place and time for holding baptisms, and the rule should not be broken without good reason.

Thirdly, baptism is a confessional act. The believer, or the Church on behalf of a child committed to its charge, confesses the faith of Jesus Christ as Lord, to use the words of what was the primitive baptismal confession. Confession is not itself the most important part of baptism, as those who are anxious to insist only on "believers' baptism" have been inclined to imply. If it were, some form of verbal declaration would be the center of the rite, rather than the washing with water. But confession of a grace received and appropriated and of a resolution to live by the Spirit do have their due place and need to be emphasized in churches where baptism is in danger of degenerating into a mere formality.

As is well known, the mode of baptism has been a matter of frequent dispute among Christians. There is no doubt that those who favor total immersion have a strong case. The practice is primitive and provides a much more vivid physical experience than sprinkling, while it effectively symbolizes the burying of the old man and his rising again with Christ. At the same time, it is not unreasonable to suggest that the rite can be modified to suit differences of climate and social habit, especially in the case of infants, and the practice of sprinkling can hardly be said to invalidate it. Sprinkling is, at least, no more of an abuse than the practice, which is widespread in Baptist churches, of using unfermented grape juice or something similar in place of wine at the Lord's Table.

The mention of infants, however, raises another and more serious issue. Is it right to baptize infants? This matter, a fruitful source of heated controversy in the past, has not had much direct discussion among theologians in recent times, but it remains one which continues to cause division between Christians who might otherwise be united and one where the issues are sufficiently confused for both sides to be anxious that full justice should be done to the other's point of view.

First, those Baptists and others who are opposed to infant baptism insist not so much on adult baptism as on what they call "believers' baptism," and they do not always regard the mode of baptism as an issue of primary importance. They deny that there is any scriptural evidence for the practice of infant baptism, and even if they allow that the question cannot be settled by proof texts but by theological principle, they go on to assert that principle demands that baptism be restricted to those who confess that Jesus Christ is Lord with the full consciousness of what that implies. The faith of the Church, or that of parents or godparents, cannot take the place of that of the individual believer. This, above all others, is a matter where each man must speak for himself. Without this emphasis on personal decision, they argue, baptism degenerates into a magical rite. It encourages an attitude contrary to the spirit of the Reformation itself because it makes people believe that they automatically become Christians in virtue of their baptism, without reference to faith. Infant baptism does not, as its defenders maintain, testify to the prevenient grace of God. It makes that grace seem arbitrary and void of content. Further-more, in those more liberal churches which no longer insist very strongly on the redemptive power of Christ, infant baptism has become more and more an innocuous and sentimental dedica-tion service, which sanctifies the natural man without repent-ance and takes all the sting and challenge out of the Christian claim in maturity.

Bald though that summary of it is, it will, at least, indicate that there is a good deal to be said for the Baptist position in this matter. That position is greatly strengthened by the fact that, even on their own principles, churches which practice in-fant baptism are guilty of a great deal of irregularity in their administration of it. Nevertheless, large numbers of churches which do not believe in automatic regeneration by baptism, and which also believe in the Reformation principle of justi-fication by faith, persist in baptizing infants. They may not always give a clear reason why they do so, but they cling tena-ciously to the practice. Nor can it be said that they do so only because of theological vested interest, buttressed in this in-stance by a pleasant and old-established social custom, power-ful though such forces are. At the time of the Reformation, when churches were not afraid to make the most radical changes if they became convinced that Scripture demanded them, they continued to baptize infants. And to this day those who have thought most about these matters are generally those who defend the practice of infant baptism most strenuously. This may be one of those parts of the Christian faith which, in Richard Hooker's famous words, may be "more true than plain."

First, those who defend the practice point out that if infant baptism is not explicitly indicated in the New Testament, neither is it explicitly forbidden. The argument from silence is never a very strong one, but as Oscar Cullmann observes in his recent reply to Karl Barth's unexpected attack on infant baptism, the fact that there is no record in the New Testament of the members of a household being baptized separately from the head of the household should carry some weight. Cullmann claims that the implication of many passages is that members of a family were considered to be Christian along with their parents. Whether that is so or not, modern defenders of infant baptism are on much surer grounds when they assert that they find justification for it in the character of the New Testament message as a whole.

For their second reason for maintaining the practice is that it takes seriously the New Testament belief in the cosmic reign of Christ. They believe that the resurrection has genuinely taken place and that it affects the terms on which all life has henceforward to be lived. All men are now born into a dispensation where Christ reigns as king. Let it be agreed that infant baptism is primarily a testimony of the faith of the parent and the Church rather than of the child. They would still want to assert that it is a proper exercise of that faith toward the child. It makes clear to the child that the Christian faith is not merely an interesting hypothesis about the nature of the universe which the Church and its parents personally find interesting and helpful, and which they would like him to consider when he reaches years of discretion, but an insight into the nature of reality which is inescapable and which makes a decisive difference to all life.

Of course they know that the child may grow up to repudiate his baptism, but if he should do so, they insist that he do so in the teeth of this assertion, made at the very threshold of his life, that he belongs to Christ and cannot understand himself or his destiny aright except in terms of the kingdom of Christ. His baptism makes clear to him his heritage as a child of God, in all its promise and responsibility, and no Christian parents can

soften its impact upon their child without confessing their own
unbelief. In baptism more is done than the dedication of a
child to Christ in the hope that in maturity he will confess
Christ for himself. It is a declaration by the parents before God
and the Church that they recognize that a child given them by
God is able to live as a child of the light and of the day from the
very beginning, because Christ's redemptive power is operative on all levels of experience, whether conscious or otherwise.
The child may choose, in later life, to work with or to fight
against the power of God. What he cannot do is to alter the
nature of things or his own Christian heritage. God does not
cease to be on the throne of the universe when men deny that
He reigns, nor does His kingship depend on human acknowledgment.

Baptist theory has never sufficiently answered this presentation of the case for infant baptism, partly, perhaps, because it
is rarely presented in this way. Baptists have ground for objection to arguments which justify infant baptism by making the
faith of godparents stand as a substitute for that of the child,
but they have never satisfactorily answered the question of the
status of the children of believers. If they belong to the Kingdom, as few Baptists would care to deny, why should they not
be accounted members of the Church, since the purpose of the
Church is to witness to and express the reality of the Kingdom
in this life? And what is the point of baptism if it is not admission to the Church? The weakness of the Baptist position is
that, partly through its commendable desire to emphasize the
importance of personal decision, it has an excessively subjec-
tivist conception of faith. This prevents it from giving enough
content to the truth that Christ reigns independently of human
feelings about Him and that there is, in F. D. Maurice's phrase,
a spiritual constitution of the universe to which it is the duty of
men to conform.

The third justification of infant baptism is that, in many instances, experience confirms its validity. Most Christians who were baptized as infants, except in those situations where baptism is indefensibly indiscriminate, have grown up as members of the household of faith from the beginning, joyfully possessing free access to their Lord who took them up in His arms and blessed them as His own. When these people come to make a clear-cut Christian decision in maturity, they do not do so as prodigals returning from the far country but as children who have always lived happily at home. They are now registering on the conscious level what they know has been true all the time. What takes place, in fact, is properly described as the confirmation of their baptism. If to a Baptist it seems unreal to baptize a puling infant, it seems no less unreal to other Christians that the great baptismal promises should be given to a young adult for whom they have been luminous realities ever since he could remember.

For these reasons, most Christians, Protestants and Catholics, believe that it is right for them to baptize their children. A further point must be made, however, which needs particularly to be remembered in these days. Baptism does not stand alone. The various ordinances of the Church belong together and make little sense without each other. It is wrong, therefore, to baptize those whose baptism can be given no content in their lives. Some people have thought that since the promises of the Gospel are universal in their application, any child upon whom the Church's hands could be laid should be baptized. But such actions lead to absurd situations, like that of those Roman Catholics mentioned by Barth who are alleged to have performed mass baptisms of American Indians with fireman's syringes.[2] The promises are indeed universal, but their sacramental seals

[2]See *The Teaching of the Church concerning Baptism* (S. C. M. Press, London, 1948), p. 52.

have meaning only in the context of the life of the Church and should not be isolated from that life. When they are, they quickly degenerate into magic and mumbo-jumbo.

That is why it is irresponsible to baptize infants concerning whom no reasonable assurance is forthcoming that they will live in any significant relation to the ordinances and common life of the Church. That does not say anything concerning the relation of those who are not baptized to the kingdom of Christ. That is a matter about which we are not required to dogmatize, and baptism is the seal of a salvation already received, not itself the reception. But it does say that the life of the Church is a unity and that one particular rite can have little meaning when wrenched from its proper context. To have children "done" and to leave it at that is simply to encourage superstition on the one hand and cynical indifference on the other. Those parents who find the rule harsh that only believing and church-associated families should have their children baptized have the remedy in their own hands. They have only to come forward and make a Christian profession themselves. It is a good rule in Western lands, where many people have an uncertain and hesitant attitude toward membership in the Church, to be very liberal in applying regulations in regard to infant baptism; but even when this is allowed for, many churches, and some of them not notably liberal in other respects, have to acknowledge great laxity in this matter.

Whatever views they may hold on the question of infant baptism, all Christians should seek to re-establish the meaning of baptism as a sacrament of the Gospel. Whether it be children or adults who are baptized, the sacrament declares the grace of God in Christ who lifts the burden and cleanses the stain of sin from mankind and enables men to live the eternal life of His children. It reminds churches in prosperous and successful communities, in particular, that they owe their strength, not to their own merit, but to God's forgiving and redeeming grace, a lesson they need constantly to relearn. It is the door to the Church, and it makes clear as nothing else does what manner of House this is and who is its Master.

CHAPTER XI

The Lord's Supper

Baptism is the sacrament of the beginning of the Christian life, the Lord's Supper of its continuance. Baptism gives to Christ's people the assurance that they are His forever, but they do not live with Him as they shall when they abide with Him in glory. They live in a world of sin, where the temptation to fall away from Christ always besets them. They need, therefore, constantly to turn back to Christ, acknowledging their failures and receiving renewed assurance of His forgiveness and of His continuing presence with them. Despite their sin and unbelief, the New Covenant has been sealed in His blood and He is in the midst enabling them to resist temptation and overcome the world. It is for this reason that, in the words of the Twenty-third Psalm, which has always had a special association with the Lord's Supper for Christians, He prepares this Table before them in the presence of their enemies, of which the greatest are their sinful selves. He gives them spiritual food to sustain them for the next stage of their pilgrimage, and this is a pledge to them that His goodness and mercy will follow them all their days and that they shall dwell in the house of their Lord forever.

Protestant thought about the Lord's Supper has always laid stress upon the gift of Christ as its determinative emphasis. The memorial of His death and the representation of His sacrifice both have their place, but they are secondary. He invites His people to meet with Him and to receive His life anew, "Take, eat, this is my body which is broken for you; this do in remembrance of me." These are the decisive words. It is true that the Church remembers His sacrifice and death, sitting round the table as the disciples did on the night in which He was betrayed, and that they are grieved anew that the sin of men and their own sin have crucified the Lord of glory. Yet the reason why this memorial is made is because He is alive and gives Himself once more as the living bread which comes down out of heaven and gives life to the world. His broken individual body has been glorified and become IIis universal spiritual body which can be divided and multiplied to meet the needs of all mankind. He is the host at this feast, and the attention of those who meet with Him is not fixed on themselves, nor even on what He has done for them in the past, but upon what He is and what He does for them here and now.

In the same way, the note of sacrifice is present in the service, but not in the sense of re-enacting the sacrifice of Calvary. That is a finished transaction between the Father and the Son, and it is not for those who benefit from it to break into that relationship and seek to add to that sacrifice by their busy importunity. That sacrifice is invoked at the beginning of divine service when, in confession of their sins, the people plead to be covered anew with the robe of the righteousness of Christ, and a sacrifice of thanksgiving is offered during the service, from which its name, the Eucharist, derives. But that sacrifice is given and made possible only because of the divine gift which comes to men as the fruit of the finished work of Christ. The offertory is a token of gratitude to Christ for His goodness and

of a determination to conform men's lives to His purpose in that
"reasonable service," that appropriate and sensible way of living, which is the consequence of the "renewing of the mind"
which they receive from Him.

What has been said of the sacramental nature of baptism is
no less true of the Supper. It is the meal, and not the elements
alone, which is sacramental: the bread broken, handed over and
eaten, the wine poured out, received and drunk, in the setting
of the fellowship and in the power of the Word. Even more
clearly than baptism, it is a corporate act, an act of the fellowship of the Church. It is the seal, not only of Christ's continuing
grace to His people, but of their continuing fellowship together
in that grace. A Protestant finds it hard to see any justification
for private masses. Most churches regard reception of the Lord's
Supper as the most distinctive act of membership, and it is
fitting that this should be so. The people of God show that they
belong to the household of faith by taking their place at the
family board. At that place, all their division from each other
falls into its subordinate position, and they know with one another the peace they receive together from their common Lord.
In one sense, the Church should always see itself as being puri-
fied, reconstituted, and renewed at every celebration of the
Lord's Supper.

Similarly, the Lord's Supper does not stand alone. It presupposes not only baptism but also the proclamation of the Word,
and its influence is meant to flow out directly into the common
life of the Church. Where it is not placed in this setting, its
function is misconceived. Either it becomes the embarrassing
adjunct of the life of the Church, which people do not quite
know what to do with, as it is in some modern Protestant
churches, or it becomes the magical, virtually self-subsistent
power which it becomes in some Catholic churches. Catholicism has much to teach most Protestant churches about the na-

ture of the sacrament and of sacramental devotion, but it also provides a warning that it can be overvalued as well as under-valued. It is one part of the life of the Church, a means of grace among others for the building up, not of individuals in their isolation, but of the whole Church in the love and service of Christ.

What, in the light of this, is "the shape of the liturgy," to use a term which the late Dom Gregory Dix has made familiar? Is there a pattern of worship for the Lord's Day to which, in its main outlines, all churches should strive to conform, even though they might vary widely as to its details, because it ex-presses the nature of the Gospel and the appropriate response to it? It is widely believed among Christians of many commun-ions in these days that there is such a pattern. It would be a great step forward toward bringing the churches together in genuine unity of heart and mind if they tried to establish it in all their chief services.

First, the members of the Church in a particular place should assemble together on the Lord's Day to wait upon their Lord. This is not a matter of whether they happen to feel like it or not, but of obligation to God and to each other. It is the act in which they recognize that they are called out of the world and gathered together into church order, as the ecclesia. When they do so, it would normally be fitting for them to make an act of praise, possibly through a hymn, in which they extol God's greatness and His redemptive goodness toward His chil-dren. This should lead them to ask God's blessing on their serv-ice and in so doing to confess their sins, in particular their unworthiness in having strayed from His ways as a Church as well as in their individual lives since last they met together. After confession, the minister should speak to them and for them the words of pardon and assurance which God has al-ready spoken in Jesus Christ. After this, the Scriptures should

be read, preferably according to a careful plan which gives due
balance to the various parts of the Bible, in Old and New Testa-
ments. The response to the readings customarily takes the form
of hymns and often of scriptural psalms and canticles. It is
appropriate that any baptisms which are called for should take
place at this point, after the initial declaration of the will and
promise of Christ in His Word and before the preaching and
the Lord's Supper. The sermon should follow, preceded by a
hymn or prayer of invocation of the Spirit. Intercession for the
needs of the Church and the world is an essential part of public
worship, and the period after the sermon, when the imagination should have been kindled and a vision of the greatness of
the divine purpose given, would seem to be a suitable time.
From this, with only sufficient break to allow those who cannot
remain to depart, the Church should proceed to the Lord's
Table.

It is false to the spirit in which God desires that His people
should serve Him to make excessively precise rules about how
the Lord's Supper should proceed. In many churches the procedure undoubtedly suffers from excessive stylization, so that
the impression is given of participation in a pageant rather
than of joining in a family meal. On the other hand, the freer
Protestant churches in particular suffer no less from a lack of
understanding of the full purpose of the service, with the result
that they oscillate between an informal barrenness and an elab-
orately inappropriate symbolism. This is regrettable because
the tradition of the Reformed churches themselves provides
guidance for the conduct of the Lord's Supper which is clear,
theologically adequate, and a good model for the emulation of
other churches.

The most suitable place from which the minister should conduct the service is behind the Table. This is not customary in
Anglican and most Roman churches, and Protestant churches

which have based their furnishings on Anglican or Roman models sometimes follow this bad example. The fact, however, that the Pope himself celebrates from behind the Table suggests that this usage is the primitive one and that there is no valid theological objection to it from the Catholic side. The minister acts in the name and place of Christ. It is desirable that as many as possible of those who share the meal should sit around the Table itself. In the Church of Scotland it is the practice to place white cloths on the tops of the pews, indicating that they are to be looked upon as extensions of the Table. It is important that the elements used and the vessels which contain them should be of the best quality available. It is not seemly that more splendid materials should be used for secular meals than for the Lord's Supper.

It is the custom in many churches to begin the service with the singing of a hymn while the people remain seated. This helps to emphasize that they are gathered round a Table and recalls the procedure in the Upper Room. The Church of Scotland, which is notable for the seemliness and impressiveness of its Communion usages, often begins the service by a procession of elders bringing in the elements, while the congregation sing a metrical version of part of the Twenty-fourth Psalm, "Lift up your heads, O ye gates." The reading of the Words of Institution is an important part of the service. To use the Scottish term again, it is the Church's "warrant" for holding the service and is its declaration of its intention to stand in the succession of the apostles, who "received from the Lord that which they delivered" unto us. From this point onward the service should follow closely the actions of Christ at the Last Supper. As He prayed, so the Church prays. Before the distribution of the elements, it has been customary from the earliest times for a great prayer of thanksgiving to be offered, in which the Church commemorates the creation of the world and the redemption of

mankind and joins its praises to those of the heavenly host who
cry, "Holy, holy, holy," round the throne of God. The words
and works of Christ, His Last Supper, His passion, death, resurrection, and ascension are recalled. Prayer is then made that
God will send His Spirit that the bread and the wine may become once more by faith the spiritual body and blood of Christ
and that God will accept the sacrifice of thanksgiving and the
offering which is set before Him. The bread is broken and dis-
tributed, the wine poured out and drunk. The precise procedure here varies from church to church, but many churches in
these days think that the symbolism of the service is weakened
if at least some of the bread is not broken and the wine is not
poured out before the congregation. After all have received,
the minister declares the peace of the Church, which expresses
the unity of the Church through renewed unity with the Lord.
In Catholic churches this is expressed by the kiss of peace
which the main participants give to each other, and in some
Protestant churches by shaking the hands of one's nearest
neighbors. The service concludes with the giving of alms for
relieving the material needs of members of the Church, with
renewed thanks and with the blessing.

It must be emphasized again that the fundamental structure
of the service is more important than uniformity of practice in
regard to details. Whether there is Epistle and Gospel in each
service or not, it is important that the Scriptures be systemat-
ically read in church. Whether intercessions come before or
after the sermon, it is essential that the public prayer of the
Church should reflect the wide range of the concerns of the
people of God. Whether or not there is leavened or unleavened
bread, or individual or common cups, or whether or not the
congregation comes forward to receive the elements or has
them brought to their seats, it is vital that the Lord's Supper
should fulfill the Lord's ordinance and show forth His death

and make available His benefits. All churches have to confess to failure in keeping the proportion of faith in this matter of the right ordering of worship, and there is no matter where they have more to learn from each other. The fact that there is no matter over which they are more conservative and suspicious of each other is a measure of their disobedience and of their need for unity in Christ.

CHAPTER XII

The Ordered Corporate Life of the Church

It has already been said that it is inadequate to think of the Word and sacraments as alone constituting the Church. The reality of the Church consists in the company of believing people to whom these are addressed and who try to live together in their light and by their power. Once stated, that is obvious enough, and it is presupposed in the teaching and practice of all the churches. Yet it is remarkable how little attention has been given, throughout the history of the Church, to defining the place which the community of Christian people has in its life.

The New Testament itself, as we have seen, has a great deal to say about the common life of God's people, but the organization of the Church seems very quickly to have fallen under the control of a clerical corporation, even though it is doubtful whether that corporation achieved its stylized classical form as quickly as most Catholic apologists maintain. This was true in East and West, but it was in the more practically minded West that the clerical dominance was most marked. In the Middle Ages it became almost complete, although it should be noted, as it is not always, that the Christian organization of the laity in relation to their daily work in cities and towns reached a level of articulation and responsibility which has rarely been paralleled since.

When the Reformation came it liberated large sections of the Church from their "Babylonish captivity" to Rome and proclaimed the freedom of the Christian man. In its early stages, however, it expressed that freedom only very inadequately in terms of church order. Luther saw the Church as primarily the *communio sanctorum* and reaffirmed the congregation as the most significant unit in its life. But insufficient content was given to the congregation's responsibility, and the need to lean on the support of the most powerful and articulate laity in the struggle with Rome—the princes—together with fear of the Anabaptists, tended to make Lutheranism in practice excessively dependent upon the clergy and upon the state.

Calvinism was more democratic in spirit than Lutheranism, and its stronger organization made it less dependent on the secular power. It succeeded in giving the congregation a much more active place in the Church's life, but this also failed to develop as it might have. It thought of the Church's life and organization too much in terms of discipline, and even though it was only in some late and decadent forms of Calvinism that that discipline took on the gloomy and repressive forms upon which popular novelists love to vent their feelings of moral superiority, its austere spirit did not directly produce that rich and joyful life which was characteristic of the New Testament community.

It was that branch of Calvinism which was most influenced by movements of Anabaptist type, the Independency, or, to use its later name, Congregationalism, of the seventeenth century, which did most to work out a positive and constructive conception of the ordered common life of the Church. Many of the small sects, some of which later grew into large churches, which arose in the seventeenth, eighteenth, and nineteenth centuries had a strong corporate consciousness and were free from clerical domination, but they often failed to relate their concerns to the wider work of the Church and to the purpose of God for all His people.

That the result of this comparative failure to give the congregation its due place in the life of the Church has been to produce an unbalanced church life is now widely acknowledged, even in some of the churches where these failings are most obvious. It is a constant Protestant criticism of Catholic churches, and in particular the Roman Catholic Church, that the imposing and coherent structure of church life presented by the hierarchy, priesthood and religious orders, conceals an inarticulate and disorganized congregational life, in which ordinary members have no function except to obey the dictates of their clerical superiors. In effect, this almost makes the clergy identical with the Church and is the most convincing argument against the Catholic claim to possess the only apostolic form of church order. But no self-critical modern Protestant would wish to set his churches upon any pedestal in this respect. Clerical domination, expressed in the cult of the popular preacher or of the minister as the managing director of the church's affairs, is nearly as widespread in some Protestant churches as it is in Catholicism, with fewer safeguards against personal eccentricities and the arbitrary use of power. In other Protestant churches, congregations have a full corporate life and a strong consciousness of their own power, but these are not ordered according to the Gospel, with the result that their churches are barely distinguishable from secular institutions.

It has already been emphasized that to stress the primacy of the congregation is not to deny the necessity for the ministry or to depreciate its importance. Karl Barth has well stated the essential point, "Jesus Christ is Lord and Saviour of the congregation as congregation. It is the congregation as the congregation which has to justify its activity to Him. The ecclesiastical order has its life solely in the congregation, but the congregation has not its life solely in the ecclesiastical order."

The word which has been translated there as "the congregation" might equally well be translated "the Christian community," and by "the ecclesiastical order" is meant what Catholicism calls the hierarchy, the various orders of ministry. There appears to be a real division between Protestantism and Catholicism at this point, although the fact that even here efforts are being made to restate both positions in terms more acceptable to the other side should not be overlooked. At the same time, the conception of an order of laity, standing over against an order of ministry in the life of the Church, which is an idea favored by ecumenically minded Catholics, is basically alien to Protestant thinking. All members of the Church are a kingdom and priests unto God. All have offices of ministry of one kind or another, and the ministry in the narrow sense is not the ultimate repository of church order but simply the essential servant of the Church's service of God. As such, the ministry has rights and responsibilities which need to be reasserted in some Protestant churches which suffer from an aggressive laicism which is at least as deadly as aggressive clericalism. But those rights and responsibilities exist within the common life of the body, which is the primary reality. The minister, it is true, represents Christ to His people in Word and sacrament, but in various ways all members of the Church represent Christ to each other, through the Spirit which dwells in their midst.

In contrast to the traditional treatment of these matters, therefore, a discussion of the ordered corporate life of the Church should start with the Christian community rather than

with the ministry. The Christian community exists in various
forms, of course: in the whole body of the great Church, in the
local congregation gathered into church order, and in units of
church life of varying sizes standing between. It is not mere
Congregationalism, however, which prompts me to suggest that
a certain priority should be given to the local congregation in
the discussion of the ordered corporate life. I freely acknowledge that Congregationalism is defective in not recognizing
clearly enough how much of the life of the Church flows
through channels other than that of the local congregation, especially in these days of mobile, centralized societies, and in
not devising sufficiently responsible organs of church government for that life. Nevertheless, in churches of all denominations the particular congregation is the most important working
unit. It is the great Church in microcosm. It is the place where
most Christians most of the time hear the Word of God and
celebrate the sacraments and seek to live in love and charity
with their neighbors.

The principle which should govern the development of
church order is that adequate organs should be devised for the
Church's responsible functioning in obedience to its Lord at
all levels of its life. In many matters, as I have already said,
the local congregation, advised by a "learned" and "gifted"
minister, is the best body for this purpose. In others, it is the
wider community of churches, whether on the civic, regional,
national, or international level. On some matters the whole
body of the Church, or a committee selected from the general
membership, should speak. On others, it should be the ministers. The attempt to find a common church order is, of course,
very important in these days when there is such a strong movement toward reunion in many churches. What is needed,
however, is not so much that some kind of synthesis should be
devised which tries to knit together strands derived from

Episcopalian, Presbyterian, and Congregationalist sources, in more or less equal proportion, as that all traditions should re-think the basis of their own church order in the light of the experience of the rest and of God's present purpose for His Church. Only in this way can a new unity be achieved wherein what each tradition has been trying to say is both judged and fulfilled.

The definition of the precise nature of such a restatement still awaits the mature deliberations of the churches, but these two points should be clear already. The first is that the past mistake of thinking of church order too exclusively in terms of the ministry must not be repeated. Whatever the rights and wrongs of the matter of episcopacy, the discussion of its merits or otherwise has been allowed to dictate the terms of thinking about the nature of church order for too long. Some Catholics, who do not yield on their conviction of the necessity of the historic episcopate to the continuance of the Church, will allow the justice of this point in these days. No satisfactory reunited Church will appear which does not achieve a new perspective on church order and which does not lay much more emphasis than most churches have yet done on the centrality of the com-mon life of the body of Christ.

The other point is that more factors than those emphasized by traditional forms of church order will have to be borne in mind in such a restatement. It is essential that the life of the Church should be ordered, but it should be ordered in such a way as to promote motion and not to arrest it. Church order has in the past undoubtedly been thought of in excessively static terms. The Church is an army on the march, not a fossil. A certain flexibility, empiricism, and provisionality are the marks of a good order for a church *in via*. Those ecclesiastical bodies who successfully evangelized the American frontier

have important lessons to teach the rest of Christendom in this
respect.

What, then, are the characteristic organs of the common life
of the Church? Certain functions in that life undoubtedly belong to the ministry, and its members should have suitable
organs, as they do in most churches, for fulfilling those functions. It is their duty to make public pronouncements concerning the definition of the Christian faith and to lay down
regulations for admission to the ministry. They should also
take counsel together to discover how best they can lead the
churches in their wider work and help each other fulfill their
ministry to particular churches. This is an appropriate function
of ministry of the Word and sacraments, but there are other
offices of ministry in the Church, variously entitled in different
churches eldership or presbyterate or diaconate. Their main
sphere of responsibility should lie in the particular congregation, but it is fitting that they should receive representation in
the wider councils of the Church, if only to provide a corrective
to any tendency towards secular professional exclusiveness and
limitation of outlook on the part of ministers of the Word and
sacraments.

Belief in the freedom of the Christian man and in the priesthood of all believers implies, however, that all members of the
Church have a responsibility for its well-being and a duty to
live in fellowship with each other. The most natural place, as
we have seen, for the ordinary member to do this is in the
local church. In many churches, however, little opportunity
is given him to do anything but attend upon the worship of
the Church and participate in various marginal activities of its
life, unless he happens to be appointed to a committee with
administrative or budgetary responsibilities. There is little place
within church order in the strict sense where his responsibility
for the well-being of the Church as Church can find adequate

expression. It is the merit of Congregational churches that, when they are true to their principles, they provide such an opportunity. This they do through their institution of the "church meeting."

This meeting is more than a meeting for dealing in a democratic fashion with business connected with the institutional aspects of the Church's life. It is a means through which the members of the Church, as the people of God in that place, strive to fulfill their common Christian calling in the light of the Gospel declared in the preaching and in the spirit of the sacramental fellowship. It should be presided over by the minister, as representative in the local church of the great Church, who is able to make available the experience of the great Church throughout the ages in helping the local church reach its own decisions. It should meet regularly. In most English Congregational churches it does so once a month, and it is a mark of degeneration when, as in most American churches, it has become merely an annual meeting at which reports are presented. Its business should be guided by the careful preparatory work and specialized knowledge of elders or deacons and others with positions of particular responsibility in the Church's life. It deals with all the ordinary matters of finance and administration which arise in any institution, but it is also a place for prayer and mutual exhortation and encouragement of a kind more intimate than that normally possible in public worship. It deals with the admission, transfer, and dismissal of members. It has the duty of seeing that adequate provision is made for the conduct of worship in all its aspects. It is a place for instruction and discussion of all matters connected with the church's well-being and for the initiating of common projects. It is not an open forum or a political assembly, but a means by which the Church in a particular place strives to reach a com-

mon mind concerning the guidance of the Spirit and to fulfill
its corporate Christian obedience.

Many of the functions performed by the church meeting are,
of course, fulfilled in other ways in most churches, but the fact
that a definite place is given within the structure of church
order itself to the common responsibility of all the members
for the well-being of the Church is of great importance. As
leaders of many other churches recognize in these days, this is a
direction in which most churches need to move. They can do
so without necessarily giving quite such all-embracing power
to the local church meeting as Congregationalism does. Many
matters are best dealt with at other levels of the Church's life,
and responsible church meetings will recognize this and accept
a limitation of their own powers in those matters where they
cannot be exercised responsibly. Furthermore, even if effective
church meetings are established in churches which do not now
possess them, this will still do no more than fill up part of what
is lacking in the life of the Church. The impact of the Church
on the wider life of society cannot be made by ecclesiastical
organizations alone. Members of churches have to obey God
in the spheres of their daily work and of their general duty in
society. To consider the large mass of complicated questions
which this raises will be the purpose of the next section.

CHAPTER XIII

The Church in Society

It will be clear from all that has gone before that the sphere of the Church's operation in the world must be much wider than that of the internal life of its members. To use New Testament language, Christ does not merely cast out the devils from within the breasts of individual church members. He also overcomes the principalities and powers and spiritual wickedness in heavenly places. Those who possess the Spirit of Christ have the power to overcome this world which, left to itself, lies in the hand of the Evil One and passes away. They are able to transform it, by the principle of internal renewal which they possess, and to give to it something of the meaning and durability of their homeland, where they shall dwell forever with God.

This transforming action must take place along the whole range of life. So far is the eschatological teaching of the New Testament from being a mere appendix to the life of the believer that it is the main source of the impulse to go out and subdue the kingdoms of this world to the dominion of God and of His Christ. Christian action in so-called secular society is, therefore, as central a concern of the Church as its worship and its internal common life. Indeed, the distinction between these is only a superficial one. The life of the Church is a unity, and no part of human life can be arbitrarily separated from the influence of the Gospel. Those Christians who, with an air of great self-conscious piety, concentrate on the cultivation of the spiritual life and ostentatiously ignore the worlds of politics, business, and educational policy as spheres of Christian decision and obedience, suffer from an inadequate Christology and deny in practice the orthodoxy which they so emphatically assert in theory. Christ is king over the real world and not merely of a small ecclesiastical enclave.

That the activity of the Church should flow out into the life of society in general is, however, one of those obvious truths which are accepted without demur by most enlightened Christians without their always grasping the full range of their implications. For example, it is a constant theme of Christian preaching that God's power is able to transform the decisive events of the natural life of man: birth, marriage, and death. Yet these are events as secular as buying and selling. As Jesus Himself said, men buy and sell, are married and given in marriage. No institution receives more veneration from the churches than the natural family, and for no part of life do they provide more specific guidance than for family life. But when economic life, and, to a lesser degree, politics or education, come into the picture, Christian teaching becomes much more hesitant and confused. This is partly due, of course, to the greater difficulty involved in discerning the will of Christ in these spheres, which makes the possibility of disagreement more acute and the need for caution more desirable. But it is also partly due to a defective understanding of the extent of the claim of Christ, which makes people assume that it is not a matter of urgent importance that they seek His will in these realms. Or if they recognize that a Christian witness needs to be made in them, they conclude that the appropriate persons to make such a witness are the clergy.

This is a serious error. Nowhere is the distortion created in the life of the Church by the preponderant influence of the clergy more obvious than in this realm. Even among the general public it is taken for granted that, for all practical purposes, the clergy are the Church. It has often been noted that when the average Englishman says about some burning current topic, "Why doesn't the Church do something?" he generally means, "Why don't the bishops say something?" Without disparaging the importance on its own level of what the bishops say, it is clearly unrealistic to suppose that the possibilities of Christian action in society are exhausted once they have spoken. It has become fashionable in our time to say that true Christian thinking is existential. God's will becomes known to men only in the encounter between God and themselves in the situation where action is demanded of them. It is the Christian doctor or factory worker or businessman or teacher who is most likely to learn God's will for his sphere of work, because he is the person who has taken the decisions for which he is answerable to God. The clergyman almost inevitably stands in a measure of detachment from most of these situations.

This is not to say that the clergyman can be of no help. On the contrary, his contribution is invaluable. He can help the Christian look at his work in a larger perspective than he is likely to be able to do on his own resources. He can indicate ways in which general Christian ideas concerning God, man, and society and the experience of the Christian past throw light on the particular matter under discussion. The very fact that he is trained to look at questions in a synoptic way can often make him help people look at their jobs in new ways and even see facts about them which they had not noticed before. Some clergy can also become so familiar with the situation in a particular sphere like education or the law or industrial relations that their opinions develop a special authority. But such cases do not affect the general rule which those few clergy who achieve the measure of *expertise* to enable them to play such roles are the first to insist upon. The man who takes the decision is the man with the responsibility for reaching it, and that responsibility should be respected by the Church. He is not the mere tool or agent of the clergy. In this realm more than most, the clergy must see themselves as "helps," who try to provide their fellow-members of the Church with the best possible equipment for fighting the Lord's battle in their own particular place.

How is this to be organized? It is one of the encouraging signs of the times that far more attention is given to this matter than in the past, although no more than a beginning has been made. Largely under the influence of the Ecumenical Movement, groups of people who have similar jobs meet together to pool experience, study together, and seek guidance together for their conduct as Christians in their daily work. Some of these meet on national and international levels, and most do so on an interdenominational basis. This is right and proper, especially for groups which do research and give leadership to others. There is, however, a spectacular need for more work of this kind to be done in local situations, where some of the findings of these research groups can be checked and applied. No neighborhood which has a strong Christian community should be without its groups of Christian doctors or teachers or trade-unionists or lawyers who are trying to help each other live responsible lives as Christians on the level of their work.

It is equally important that these activities should be seen as church activities. It is true that it is often best that they should not be activities of particular congregations but of the whole Christian community of a neighborhood, and it is of great importance that their procedure and form of organization should be determined by the character of the work they do rather than by ecclesiastical institutionalism. It is even more important that they should not be obstructed from devoting time and energy to these matters because of claims upon their time and energy made by clergy for more immediate service of the sanctuary in the way of Sunday-school work or church committees. But when all these qualifications are made, it remains essential that those who engage in these activities should see them as being of one piece with what they do in Church and see the means of grace and the fellowship of the Church as food for sustaining them in Christian obedience in the worlds of their secular callings. Only thus can the missing half of the Church's life be filled up and a new and more healthy relationship emerge between the clergy and the services of the Church on the one hand and the ordinary members and their real lives on the other.

This side of the Church's life has gone by default for so long that few people have much experience of how to conduct themselves in dealing with it. There are, however, a few points about how such activity should proceed which are now clear, and to mention them may help those who embark upon it with little previous experience to avoid costly errors.

First, a great deal of humility is needed on the part of all concerned. This may seem trite, but it is not. All churchmen suffer from the occupational defect of preferring spectacular and dramatic action to effective action where Christian obedience in society is concerned, and the tendency to high-flown eloquence of the sermonic type becomes the more pronounced in proportion to the magnitude of the task involved. Too much so-called Christian witness in society is a matter of what Dr. Carnegie Simpson has described as lying on one's back at the foot of the mountains and saying fine things about the peaks. It is good occasionally to look at the peaks, but Christians in society are rarely in danger of forgetting them, especially if there are clergymen in the group. Most of the time of Christian groups in this realm should be spent in mapping out the country between their position and the peaks and in trying to establish firm camps in the foothills. In fact, it is a good rule, especially in groups under clerical leadership, that before overt theological principles are discussed a great deal of time should be spent in discussing the nature of the jobs which the members of the group perform and the places where they are conscious of the pressure of decision. Only when that has been done can much realism be given to the attempt to submit their assumptions about their jobs to critical Christian examinations. Clergy must exercise a self-denying ordinance here and train themselves to listen. They have their pulpits. The first voices to be heard in discussion of Christian responsibility in daily work are those of the persons who have to make decisions in these fields.

Secondly, the highest standards of professional competence are demanded of Christian discussion of these matters. It may be partly the result of the pietist cult of emotional spontaneity in dealing with religious matters, but it is a fact that on the comparatively rare occasions when Christians discuss a technical matter connected with their work they often assume that to discuss it in a Christian way means to do so in a vague and generalized way with undue reference to subjective considerations which are not always relevant to the matter in hand. One reason why talk about "Christians in industry" or similar subjects is distrusted by those in industry is that people have a shrewd suspicion that some of those who speak thus are more interested in trying to salve their consciences or to strike attitudes than to ensure that the right job is done in the right way.

It is ominous that so many Christian laymen's groups should be so largely composed of people in the advertising business. Christian action in society is not a form of window-dressing, which tries to assure unsympathetic critics how socially enlightened and active the churches are and which is at great pains to see that institutions with Christian labels receive full credit for any work done. It is a matter of obedience to the will of God, the only source of life and health for individuals and societies. The most necessary Christian virtues in this field are the most unspectacular. Patience, forbearance, moderation, and, above all, the undervalued virtue of the disciplined application of cold and honest intelligence, are infinitely more important than the ability to make a dramatic gesture or to make a quotable pronouncement. These latter are the instruments of Communist propaganda, and the Communists use them because they believe that it is only in this life that men have their rewards.

Perseverance is not the least of the undervalued Christian virtues in this realm. Most worldly prizes can be won only by hard work and struggle, but Christians are tempted to assume that the profession of Christian ideals is enough to ensure their fulfillment. Christian groups love to launch crusades with ambitious plans to reform society, only to flag and lose interest once obstacles are encountered or when it becomes obvious that the need is not so much for dramatic as for steady and painstaking action. The gift of perseverance is one of the rarest and most valuable gifts of the Spirit, and without it, Christian witness in society will continue to retain its adolescent character, and purposeful and hardheaded men, dedicated to the unremitting pursuit of their own selfish ambitions, will continue safely to ignore it.

Two points of a more general nature remain to be made. The first is that when more of the Church's attention is directed to fulfilling Christ's will in daily life and less to its own institu-

tional development, the character of the Church's internal life
will undergo many changes. Many Christian people who have
developed a critical concern for the fulfillment of their duty
in politics or education or industry or the professions have begun to look at theology and the services of the Church with
fresh eyes and to expect different things from their clergy.
While making the real work of the clergy emerge as being even
more essential, it will expose the pretensions which some clergy
make for themselves and their office. The vexed question of
conflicting clerical claims, for example, which does so much to
hold up the progress of reunion, will probably never be resolved unless the voices of the laity, in responsible fulfillment of
their own vocation in the Church, are made much more articulate. It will also intensify the need for real Christian fellowship,
not as a leisure-time occupation of the suburban family but on
the level of the job, where the need is greatest and the possibilities of meeting it the richest.

The other point is that a great deal of what has been said in
this chapter applies only in the free societies of the Western
world. Christians in totalitarian countries have very different
problems and opportunities. Those confronting Christians in
Eastern countries, where they are only a tiny minority of the
population and are often nationals of foreign countries, may
have more points of affinity with those of the West, but they
are still very different. To try to analyze them would be beyond
the scope of this book and the competence of its writer, but it
is important to remember that they exist and that the task of
the Church in society is always very largely conditioned by the
kind of situation with which its members have to deal.

CHAPTER XIV

Church and State

It was said at the beginning that the Church was the strangest institution in existence, strange in its persistence and in its power of internal renewal. There is another great institution which is not so strange, but which alone rivals the Church in its persistence and in the quality of the loyalty it evokes, and that is the State. It is true that particular states come and go and that none of them can claim the continuity which the various forms of the Church possess. But the State in one form or another appears to be universal and indispensable. When the organization of the State breaks down in any but the most rudimentary form of society, an intolerable situation arises and it has quickly to be re-created. Anarchy is not a possible form of human society for more than the briefest interlude. Marxists speak of the gradual withering away of the State when the classless society dawns after the dictatorship of the proletariat. Christians, with more realism, reserve such a possibility for the final Day of the Lord.

The first point which needs to be grasped in Christian thinking about the Church's relation to the State is this of the State's

permanence and inescapability. Churches cannot avoid having
dealings with it, except at the price of social insignificance.
That may seem obvious enough, and it should be to anyone
with any sense of history, but it is something which some
churchmen have shown a curious reluctance to accept. Those
powerful churches which have been deeply influenced by
Pietism and Revivalism, and which are commonly called the
Free Churches, have many members who insist vociferously
that it is both possible and desirable for Church and State to
have practically nothing to do with each other and many more
members who wish to have their dealings with each other kept
to the barest minimum.

Such an attitude, at least in its simpler forms, derives whatever measure of plausibility it possesses, not from any close
study of Scripture or of the human situation in general, but
from a peculiar set of social circumstances which are rapidly
passing away. In the United States and in the British Domin-
ions, which are the countries where this notion has had its
widest currency, people were so busy opening up new frontiers
that they did not have to trouble very much about defining
carefully the relation of one institution to another. They rarely
got in each other's way, and when they did there were principles ready to hand, those of liberal individualism, which
justified the utmost suspicion of the State's activities in ecclesiastical as in economic matters, although, very curiously, the
same suspicion did not extend to the fundamental matter of
education. It was this situation which made the slogan "a free
Church in a free State" the expression of a simple and emi-
nently practicable ideal. As an ideal it may possibly have
permanent validity, but it is naïve indeed to imagine that what
it means will always be so clear as to need little discussion
and that it can normally be fulfilled without serious effort.

The second counsel of wisdom in regard to Church and State

is to have in mind how the relation between them constantly changes and how important it is, therefore, to keep open the question of its redefinition. This is true even in considering the way in which the experience of the Church in the Bible in relation to the State provides guidance for the present time. The world view of many New Testament writers, notably Paul, presupposed that the affairs of "this present age" were under the domination of certain "powers," which lacked absolute authority but were permitted by God to exercise a measure of control over human affairs. When Paul spoke, therefore, of the "powers that be" and of their being "ordained of God," he was not necessarily conferring a special sanctity and inviolability upon them. He was recognizing what so many modern Free Churchmen are reluctant to recognize, that the State exists in the providence of God as a reality in the spiritual order and that the believer has to come to some kind of terms with it. When he went on further to speak of the State as a minister of God's righteousness, he was speaking specifically of the Roman Empire as he had known it. He was not giving a comprehensive approval to the State in all its forms, as some Christians have imagined. The fact that it was possible from the earliest times for Christians to take a different view of the State is proved by the Book of Revelation, which was written against the background of a persecution of the Church by the Roman Empire itself.

Unless the particular circumstances of the New Testament in relation to the State are borne in mind, thinking about the State today is exposed to two grave dangers. The first is that the possibilities of corruption inherent in the modern State are not clearly enough recognized. This is true not only of countries which have national churches, although the oft-quoted example of Lutheran Germany in the last hundred years is a sufficiently vivid reminder of the reality of the danger in such cases, but

also of all communities where the State has great prestige and
is a powerful center of unity and meaning for men's lives. The
other danger is one which arises on the opposite side. Because
the Roman Empire, relatively just though it may have been,
was a pagan state and the attitude of Jesus and Paul toward it
was one of little more than neutrality, modern Christians may
be disinclined to think as positively and constructively as they
should about the situation of a State where the Christian faith
is widely acknowledged and churches have a great deal of
influence and where many Christian individuals may hold positions of authority in the service of the State.

These dangers must be avoided because, unless the Church
succeeds in working out a right relation to the State, not only
can the State destroy the Church as an effective visible institution but it can also destroy human freedom and dignity in the
same process. One of the most obvious and ever-present facts
of the twentieth century has been the immense extension of the
range and influence of the nation-state. Forces stronger than
the conscious wills of individuals and parties have brought this
about, although these may have done much to help or hinder
them. The nature of modern industrial organization and com-
munications are such that they appear almost inevitably to
drive society to become more centralized and its parts to become more interdependent. The need for control of this intri-
cate machine becomes more and more urgent because the risk
of breakdown is always growing and the consequences of
breakdown are becoming more far-reaching. This means that
the power of the State over men's lives extends itself, and with
that the temptation to the strong-willed and covetous to use
that power for their own purposes, often at the expense of rival
states. This produces war, which, in its turn, greatly intensifies
the process of centralization.

The demonic possibilities of this situation have been vividly

actualized in totalitarian countries. In these countries, churches
have been forced to see that they have to fight for their own
life and for all the distinctively human values. That fight goes
on in many countries at the present time, and its outcome is
still uncertain. It is watched anxiously by churches in other
countries more fortunately placed. What these churches do not
always see, however, is that the challenge of the modern nation-
state confronts them also, and that they are misusing their opportunity if they imagine that the less acute form in which it
presents itself to them means that they have no serious problem.

Those churches who believe themselves to be in this situation have an attitude over ecclesiastical matters which is not
unlike that of those businessmen and politicians who, in dealing with their own affairs, believe that they can preserve freedom of action for the individual by minimizing political control
or regulation of business activity. What they fail to see is that,
under the conditions of the modern world, this means that
business interests dictate the terms of life to the rest of the
community, that the economically weak go to the wall, and
that the non-economic factors in public life are ignored. In so
far as countries are able to maintain some reality in slogans
like "a free Church in a free State," it is because other factors
in their life, whose strength they are taking for granted, are
able to maintain a precarious balance between the power of
the churches and that of the State and other strong interests
in society.

That is an exceedingly fortunate situation in which to be in
the modern world, and it is not likely to continue indefinitely
without a great deal of careful handling. Churches in these
nations, such as America and most of the British Commonwealth, are still sufficiently strong to compel a measure of respect for their right to exist and to operate freely on their own

terms. They have also learned, whether rightly or wrongly, to achieve acceptable compromises with the State over contentious matters such as education, military service, marriage laws, and the conduct of economic life. Let either of these conditions alter and the problem of the relation of Church and State is likely to become difficult and acute. To imagine that the relation is satisfactorily settled once for all and need occasion no further anxiety is the surest way to precipitate a crisis.

It will already be clear that this is not to say that the way forward for the churches must be only one of intense suspicion of the State and vigilant determination to assert their independence at every possible opportunity. Churches do right to be suspicious of the State, especially when it comes bearing gifts, but such a negative attitude is by itself a totally inadequate response to the present situation. The Church has a positive duty toward the State, a duty which is made the more imperative by two special considerations which apply to the free societies of the West.

The first consideration is that many Christian men serve the State, in a way which was never true in New Testament times, and they require guidance as to how they should do it in a Christian way. This becomes an issue whether a state calls itself formally a Christian one or not and whether there is an established church or not.

The other consideration is that there is no reason to suppose that the State cannot be made to serve the glory of God and the true welfare of mankind like any other human institution. Indeed, the vast extension of the State's power in the modern world makes it all the more essential that it should be redeemed, because the consequences of failure to do so will be all the more disastrous. Here is a place where slogans which are, perhaps, too glibly used by Christian speakers do, in fact, soberly apply. The alternative for the State is Christ or chaos.

The good and the evil ripen together unto the Day of Judgment in human affairs. To the extent to which the evil ripens, it can be overcome only by the developing power of the good. The great powers which have been unleashed by modern science and technology, which have so vastly enlarged the sphere of human decision and made the political question so urgent, can be subdued only by those who genuinely possess and make use of the powers of the age to come. The prospect of dominion which the modern state gives tempts the demons which lie within all states to come forward and claim it. Their challenge has to be met by those who claim to live under the dominion of Christ, and they must seek to assert His Lordship over them.

That is New Testament language which may seem strange and remote to modern ears, but it gives a clear directive to Christians in their relations with the modern state. They must not submit passively to anything the State chooses to do, justifying themselves with a quietist misinterpretation of the teaching of Jesus and Paul. Nor must they regard the State as always and of necessity an unclean monster, the beast from the abyss, with which they must avoid being contaminated at all costs. Nor yet must they interpret establishing Christ's dominion over the powers of the State in the sense of seeking to make the Church, or a quasi-ecclesiastical Christian prince, lord over the State. This is a temptation into which the Roman Catholic Church is constantly prone to fall and into which other churches are sometimes ensnared at various times in their history when they enjoy great power. The churches must help the State to understand its true function in the Christian dispensation. They must make its officers realize the dangers inherent in the unlimited exercise of power and make available the resources of Christian insight in helping them to avoid these dangers. They must preach a doctrine of man and society in

Christian terms which is relevant to the day-to-day decisions
which Christian men have to take in administering the State.
Above all, while maintaining a sharp distinction between
Church and State, they must inspire the State with a vision of
a free and godly commonwealth which will enable it to organize itself to serve human welfare and not merely to act as a
"dyke against sin."

This clearly involves an attitude to the State much wider
than any which can be expressed simply in terms of the relations between church institutions and governments. These relations are important enough on their own level, but it is usually
a secondary level. Churches can enjoy excellent relations with
governments and yet fail badly in fulfilling their Christian responsibilities to the State, and they can do so just as much in
free England or America as they can in Franco's Spain. How
this wider responsibility will express itself will vary greatly
from one situation to another. There is no ideal Christian attitude to the State, as though Church, State, and community
were static entities instead of living realities which were constantly shifting their ground in relation to each other. There
are some general observations which can be made, however,
about how Christians should conduct themselves in relation to
states where they have the possibility of effective influence
upon their policies.

The first is that in defining Christian duty in the modern
state, and the more specific issue of the relations between
Church and State, the initiative must come from the churches,
and that, in practice, generally means the clergy. Where a
measure of goodwill toward the churches exists on the part of
statesmen, in countries where professing Christians are in a
majority, it is obviously the duty of churchmen to define the
kind of relationship to the State which they find most satisfactory and which the State is likely to find acceptable. Further,

since most of the opposition to such proposals on behalf of a particular church is likely to come from other churches, it should be a rule that they should settle their differences among themselves before allowing them to enter the political arena. This is the course of wisdom and expediency as well as of Christian responsibility. When churches discuss issues of this kind together, due weight can be given to the theological factors involved, as well as to all the political, in an atmosphere of understanding. When churches can agree, even if a compromise has been reached, they may be reasonably confident in most Western nations that statesmen will be ready to accept their proposals gratefully, since there is no matter which a sensible politician is more reluctant to touch than ecclesiastical controversy. Many matters of considerable moment for the future well-being of churches and nations go by default for this very reason.

This may seem a very innocuous suggestion to make, but it has, in fact, very important consequences. The problem of trying to find a more explicitly Christian basis for public education in the United States, for example—a matter of the utmost importance for the future of the nation—is almost hopelessly bedeviled by interdenominational suspicion, to the grave detriment of all the churches, Protestant and Catholic, as well as to that of the educational system itself. No politician with any concern to be re-elected is ever likely to touch such a contentious issue of his own volition, so that unless the churches take the initiative in trying to break the deadlock between them, the current interpretation of the first amendment of the Constitution will remain unchallenged and the secularized character of public education in the most churchgoing country in the world will become more and more pronounced.

On the wider matter of Christian influence in public affairs, it is essential to see that this is not primarily a matter for any

church organizing itself as a pressure group. Such tactics may
occasionally be necessary over a particular issue, but they are
dangerous and should always be temporary and concerned
with strictly limited objectives. The primary responsibility of
the clergy in particular in this realm is not to strive to obtain
the best terms possible for the churches as institutions from the
State in such matters as official recognition or tax exemption,
nor even to throw their weight into the balance in trying to
make politicians accept certain policies, but to help the statesmen become better statesmen in the sight of God. It makes a
great difference to the Christian engaged in politics if he can
regard his church not as another pressure group to be assuaged,
nor as a certifying agency for his moral respectability, but as
a source of personal counsel and encouragement and occasional
rebuke, where he can share his many difficult moral problems
with people who, on that level, have no particular axe to grind
and seek only to help him. The pastoral function of the ministry
in relation to politicians has been much neglected, yet it is a
far more constructive contribution to Christian influence in
politics than any number of resolutions or pronouncements of
church assemblies.

Secondly, the most effective way in which churches as institutions can influence political life is not by forming Christian
political parties, at least in English-speaking lands, but by setting an example in the way in which they conduct their own
internal affairs. Many of the problems which confront the State
in the modern world have their counterparts in the institutional life of the churches. They, too, have to face the difficulties of "democracy face to face with hugeness," of seeking
to retain the human measure in an increasingly centralized and
swift-moving society, and of finding place for individual enterprise in the midst of large, closely knit organizations. If the
churches can show that they are able to surmount these diffi-

culties in their own affairs, the State will not be slow to heed them, and its taking heed will not be the less effective for being unconscious.

History provides several illustrations of how this works. For example, the procedure of the British House of Commons and of the Trade Union Movement owes a great deal to that of ecclesiastical assemblies of different kinds, and the influence of New England Congregationalism on American political institutions is strong. Today, however, churchmen often give the impression that they are full of good advice for the planning of society in general, often with little sense of political realities, while they remain cheerfully haphazard in the conduct of their own affairs. That is not a responsible Christian approach to politics.

Thirdly, it is more important that this more constructive attitude toward the State should find expression on the personal level rather than on that of official relations. As we have already seen, nothing is easier than for Church and State to make formal gestures of mutual acknowledgment which conceal fundamental tensions. This is not to say that such gestures have no value. Most British people would say that their experience shows that they matter a great deal. Apart from anything else, the legislative program of most states in these days is so all-embracing that churches can be greatly hampered in their work almost by inadvertence. A severe blow can be struck at churches, for example, if a government department makes an order that reservists should do military training on Sunday mornings.

At the same time, as perhaps British or, at least, English experience also shows, it is essential that the distinction between Church and State should be sharp and clear on the institutional level. In England it is not always clear whether it is the Church of God or the British nation which is speaking.

Churchmen should express an active responsibility toward the State, but they must be free to speak prophetically to it and, if need be, to imperil the State's security in the name of God. It is fitting that in a predominantly Christian society the State should be encouraged to express that love and tolerance and care for the weak and defenseless which should always be found in the Church, but it must never be forgotten that it remains the State, a dyke against sin, and that the policeman is always in the offing. Even if he is in the service of the best of states, the churchman must always be conscious of the fact that he has a dual allegiance and the two loyalties will frequently pull in different directions. Apart from anything else, the character of states changes, and it will be hard for the Church to disentangle itself from a state which has gone off after alien gods if it has not been careful to retain its own distinctive freedom.

Finally, churchmen should possess a strong sense of urgency in encouraging each other to take an active and responsible part in the affairs of all the states where they have freedom to do so in a Christian way. The opportunity may not be available indefinitely. Terrific responsibilities weigh upon the shoulders of those who have to administer states in these days of the upheaval of nations and of atomic warfare. The moral cost of modern society is very high, and it is those at the centers of power who have to meet most of the bills. It would be a grave dereliction of duty if the churches did not equip their members to the best of their ability to serve the State in these days and if they did not support them with every resource of prayer and sympathy and knowledge.

CHAPTER XV

The Unity of the Church

Unity is a mark of the true Church of Christ. Christ is our peace and we are one family in Him. He has united His people, Jew and Gentile, in one body upon the tree. Those who possess His Spirit are reconciled to God and to each other, and are ambassadors to men of that reconciling grace. The purpose of church order is to build up the body of Christ in love so that His members attain not to isolated self-sufficiency but to a common perfect manhood. The purpose of the whole economy of salvation is to sum up all things in Christ and to enable mankind to share in the unbroken communion which the Son holds with the Father.

The message of the New Testament could not be clearer than it is upon this point. The fact that the society which knows this unity and which exists to testify to its reality and to bring it to a divided mankind is, nevertheless, itself divided is all the more scandalous and indefensible. This is the most damaging of all reproaches to the good name of the Church of Christ, and that it is so familiar and of such long standing certainly does not make it any the less disgraceful. To acquiesce in this situa-

tion is to deny the name of Christ. It is true that divisions are
now so well established and have such complex ramifications
that only some of them hold any immediate prospect of being
broken down. Most people now living can hardly hope to see
more than a partial restoration of the visible unity of Christ's
people upon earth. The road to unity will certainly be long and
exhausting. In some cases it may be so overgrown as to appear
not to exist at all. But the will to unity and the refusal to rest
content in disunity must remain and strive to find expression
if any individual or church is to continue to be faithful to the
intention of the Lord of the Church.

Some churches contrive to avoid the tension which this situation creates by denying that the Church is divided. They hold
that they themselves constitute the true Church, and that those
who do not accept them as such are either schismatics or here-
tics who must be held responsible for their continued separa-
tion from the true Church. The Roman Catholic Church is, of
course, the most obvious example of a church holding this
position, but it is also held in less explicit forms by other
churches as well, not least by small Protestant sects who are
acutely conscious of the distinctive purity of their own belief
and practice. The position of the churches of the Orthodox East
appears, to a Western mind, to be ambiguous in this matter,
since they combine frequent assertions of a position not unlike
that of Rome with participation in ecumenical activities with
other churches.

Other churches avoid this tension in a quite different way.
They deny that visible unity between churches on the institutional level matters very much. They take the view that
churches are all going the same way, although by different
roads. As long as they are all reasonable, tolerant, and charita-
ble toward each other, do their differences of teaching and
organization matter very much? This attitude, which is wide-

spread among members of the more liberal churches, may
have its elements of truth, but it is open to the charge that it
has a very impoverished conception of what the unity which is
in Christ means, and a consequent lack of understanding of the
damage inflicted upon the cause of Christ by the complacent
readiness of churches to go their own way in virtual indifference to each other.

Most churches in Christendom, at least as far as their most
articulate and responsible spokesmen are concerned, now regard it as their duty to live in this tension and not to try to
escape from it. Those churches who met for the first assembly of
the World Council of Churches at Amsterdam in 1948 an-
nounced that they were resolved "to stay together," and this
was a declaration of their determination never again to acquiesce in a state of division. It also implied that they were no
longer concerned to make absolute claims for their own denominations. It is true that many of the churches which belong
to the World Council firmly believe that they hold in trust
spiritual treasures which other churches must accept before
they can hold full communion with them. Most Anglicans feel
this about episcopacy, and the Orthodox churches feel the same
about the whole tradition of Orthodoxy. But they all recognize
those who differ from them on these matters, while they remain
united with them over others no less fundamental, as fellow-
Christians and as, in some sense, fellow-members of the Church.
All who participate in the World Council believe that disunity is
a sin for which all churches, in varying degrees, are responsible,
that other churches emphasize parts of Christian truth and
life which they have neglected and that they have shown a
Christian interest for people and regions which they have
ignored. They believe, therefore, that they are being disobedient to the Head of the Church unless they renew fellowship

with each other and strive to do together all things except those which conscience compels them to do separately.

It is important to see the Ecumenical Movement in the light of considerations such as these. This movement, which has been gathering momentum in most of the non-Roman churches of the world for the last half century, is not merely a means for promoting the organizational reunion of the various denominations, although that is certainly part of its purpose. It is also, and more fundamentally, a means by which divided churches, partial in vision and limited in influence, express their common responsibility to that great Church in which they have part, the Church in the purpose of God as we have tried to consider it in the course of this book. The Greek root of the work "ecumenical" means "the whole inhabited earth." Its meaning is, therefore, very close to that of the word "catholic," and it is used partly because it lacks the specific association which "catholic" has with one section of the Christian community. In the provisional and mobile state of relations which the churches participating in the movement have with each other, there is merit in the very vagueness and generality of the term.

Churches have gone their separate ways for so long that it is often hard for them to know how to proceed, and there are many aspects of the divine purpose for the whole Church which they have yet to explore. The aim of this movement is to help them, even in the midst of their divisions, to express more fully the life of the one Christ in His body. They do this by waiting together upon the Spirit through common study, discussion, and prayer, that they may learn a less imperfect knowledge of God's will. They also do it by mutual aid, by common social witness, and by planning a common strategy of evangelism, as well as by promoting institutional reunions of particular churches whenever that is possible. The way in which the World Council undertakes these tasks may, of course, be open to criticism in detail, but the task to which it sets itself is surely clearly laid upon all the churches by the Lord of the Church. It is hard to see how Christian bodies can hold themselves aloof from it and yet claim to be obedient to Christ.

This is much more than a matter of technical and exclusive conferences between theologians and church leaders, which are the activities of the Ecumenical Movement which receive most publicity. These are an essential part of the movement's life, whose importance the impatient activist may be inclined to underrate, but their results for ordinary church life are, for the most part, indirect, and it is reasonable to assume that their findings, so far as they are relevant to the average church member's concerns, will be transmitted in a suitable form by the representative of the great Church in the local church, his own minister. The movement itself is much wider than the World Council of Churches or the various national or regional councils of churches which are to be found in most countries. The custom of some churchmen of speaking of activities as ecumenical when they are merely interdenominational or international is seriously misleading. Such activities are "ecumenical" only when they express a responsible concern for the wholeness of Christ's purpose in the world and that concern can find expression on all levels of the Church's life.

Indeed, for the ordinary Christian, who is rarely likely to attend an interdenominational, let alone a world-wide, gathering, the chief sphere of ecumenical activity is his own local church itself. It is possible to have an ecumenical, as distinct from a sectarian, attitude toward the internal life of a particular denomination and of a particular local congregation as well as toward its external relations. Here indeed is the main battleground of the Ecumenical Movement in these days, and its front-line troops are not secretaries of interdenominational organizations, indispensable though their onerous labors are, but

the ministers of particular churches in their day-to-day contacts
with their people.

To achieve internal ecumenicity, a local church should strive
always to put first things first. This is a more difficult and more
fundamental task than it sounds. The particular church's temptation is always to put its own theological or liturgical or social
traditions, or its interest in the secular well-being of its local or
national community, above its duty to the great Church and
to forget that its function is to be "the outcrop of the great
Church in a particular place." It will resist the temptation to
become a church of the *pagani,* worshiping its own local gods
and giving undue veneration to its own particular ancestors. Its
primary possessions are not those things which are distinctive
to it but those which it holds in common with the rest of the
Church: the Bible, the Gospel sacraments, the ordered corporate life, the apostolic ministry. It will dispose of its resources, whether of time or money or spiritual ability, not
simply with a view to promoting its own success in its own immediate neighborhood but in terms of the contribution it is best
equipped to make to the whole Church. It will accept its
obligation to exercise a ministry of reconciliation not only to
those who live in its vicinity who are not reconciled to God but
also to those other Christians who are gathered together into
church order under different denominations in its own place.
It will always be open to the possibility that the living God will
call it forward to new ventures of faith and possibly to the painful task of uprooting itself and starting its work elsewhere. Involved with the life of its own community as it will be, it will
yet live in it as not being of it. It will testify to those who are
about it that the people of God are pilgrims and that their
home is not here, even in the places they themselves call home,
but with Christ.

The wider work of the Ecumenical Movement depends on

this internal ecumenicity of the particular congregation much more than is commonly realized. Church leaders are obviously only able to go forward a little ahead of those they lead, and they badly need the intelligent and informed support of their people in such matters. Otherwise the most enlightened and responsible policies for the future well-being of all the people of God will founder on the rock of the suspicion and indifference of the great majority of church people who have not taken the trouble to understand them. The need to do so is particularly urgent in these days because the field of Christian action which cannot be undertaken by the local congregation alone is vast. The modern world is on the march, whether the Church is or not, and Christians must move fast and into new places if they are to keep up with it. People change their place of residence constantly and, in the most characteristic countries of the modern world, vast programs of church extension have to be carried out. They find much of their common life not in the neighborhood where the local church is but in the great institutions of the modern world—universities, corporations, armies, factories, hospitals—and into these the Church has to follow them. Churches in other lands are persecuted or suffer because of war and need help for resistance or rebuilding, quite apart from the ongoing and ever-changing work of missions. Specialized agencies have to be created for dealing with all these matters.

That this should be so is sometimes deplored by conservative Christians, who prefer a neater and more compassable form of church organization, but such an attitude has little to justify it. The fact that the world is changing and that the Church is changing with it has its evils and dangers but it is also a sign of vitality in both. A static situation also has its evils and dangers, which are the more deadly for not always being so clearly visible. It is essential that churchmen should approach this situation as constructively as possible, without begrudging any support they are able to provide for these wider activities of the churches and without sighing for the return of a more "normal" pattern of church life. More of the total resources of all the churches are having to go into these activities than ever before, and they should be seen not as marginal affairs which need be supported only when more important matters, generally connected with the internal life of congregations, are attended to, but as integral to the Church's existence in the world of today. It is a great step forward that so many of these activities are organized on an interdenominational basis and with a clear ecumenical reference.

The question of reunion between separated denominations is also integral to the life of the churches and not a marginal pursuit of enthusiasts. Let it be admitted that to be dazzled by the vision of one great reunited church, embracing all Christians, and worthy to be called "The Holy Catholic Church," as the immediate aim of ecumenical planning, is to be out of touch with realities. Even if, *per impossibile,* such a church were to come into being in the near future, its creation would involve problems of adjustment so immense as to absorb all the energies of most leading churchmen for many years and leave no opportunity for dealing with other urgent matters, such as evangelism and the need to strive for a more responsible society in a world dominated by the fear of atomic war. Also, if past experience is any guide, it can be confidently predicted that as soon as such a church came into being the Spirit would confound its pretensions by prompting new dissident groups into existence.

The way of progress toward reunion is obviously that of proceeding step by step, giving movements toward reunion the high degree of priority they deserve but keeping them in due proportion in relation to the overruling purpose of God. In some situations, and as between some particular churches, the achievement of organic reunion immediately is obviously their Christian duty and they should press forward toward it. In others, and as between others, reunion may not be immediately practicable, but duty to the whole Church demands active co-operation in many common projects and the clearing of the ground before approaching greater unity. The progress made between churches in both these directions in recent years under the impulse of the Ecumenical Movement has, in fact, been very remarkable. The number of organic unions achieved makes an impressive list.[1] Even when they are unions between closely related denominations the element of self-transcendence involved in their accomplishments should not be minimized. The vested interest which a well-established denomination builds up in its own continuance is very great, and the inertia and resistance to change of the great mass of its members is formidable. Even the simplest form of reunion, like that accomplished a quarter of a century ago by the divided branches of the Methodist Church in England, is a considerable spiritual achievement, and reunion between more widely divergent denominations, like that made in South India, is a notable triumph of grace. Such achievements are not without analogy to the voluntary surrender of sovereignty by an independent nation to a larger whole.

There are other churches, however, with which it is impossible to enter into direct discussion of reunion, whether immediate or only remotely prospective, but which affect the activities of churches which belong to the World Council and toward which they cannot avoid taking up an attitude as Christians. Most prominent of these in Western lands is, of course, the Roman Catholic Church. This church gives every encouragement to those Christians who do not submit to its exclusive claim to adopt an attitude as unecumenical as its own in their

[1]See *Church Unity, 1937–1952,* by Stephen Neill (Harper, New York).

dealings with it. Yet, although at many places it is necessary
to say "No" to Roman Catholic pretensions, the temptation to
adopt a purely negative attitude must be resisted. Rome holds
too many souls in trust, she brings forth too many authentic
fruits of the Spirit and she is too great a social and political fact,
for it to be possible to treat her responsibly in this way. Whether
she or they like it or not, she has to have dealings with other
churches and has to define some kind of attitude toward them.
This is obviously true in America, where it is a matter of vital
importance to the future of the nation that Rome and the other
churches should work out a constructive *modus vivendi,* but it is
true in most other Western lands as well. Her absence from the
assemblies and committees of the World Council does not mean
that she can go her own way unaffected by its existence, any
more than the Roman priest can ignore the Protestant minister
on Main Street or on the college campus.

On the contrary, the rise of the Ecumenical Movement confronts Rome with her greatest crisis since the Reformation, and
her future largely depends on the way in which she responds
to it. For the first time she is confronted by the immense
strength of the non-Roman Christian world, far greater than
her own once it is organized, united in seeking to define what
they mean by the Catholic Church and trying together to realize more effectively the Church's universal mission. Rome may
very well react to this challenge by becoming even more defen-
sive than she is at present. Her whole tradition encourages her
in such a course. But non-Romans should note very carefully
the fact that there are courageous and powerful voices raised
within the Roman Church, in France and in other lands,[2]
which urge her to accept this challenge and put out her talent

[2]See the American Roman Catholic periodical, *Cross Currents,* which appears, to a Protestant, to have a genuinely ecumenical approach to the
mission of the whole Church.

to usury in the commerce of the Ecumenical Movement, in the belief that that is the only way to prove its worth. How far they are likely to be successful may be a very open question, but Christians in other communions who have a genuine longing for the unity of all Christ's people have no right to discourage them by taking it for granted that conversation with Rome is a waste of time.

Nor should it be overlooked that, although Rome makes it her business to present a façade of inviolability to the world, she does, in fact, change her position quite radically from time to time. In the turbulent and rapidly moving modern world, Rome may change a great deal, perhaps in despite of herself. The great increase of American influence within the Roman Church, for example, is not likely to leave her unaffected. To write her off as lost as far as the Ecumenical Movement is concerned would be shortsighted as well as irresponsible and provincial. She may come to an ecumenical temper in her own way rather than in ours, but it is an act of unbelief in the power of the Holy Spirit to assume that she will never come or that we can do nothing to help her do so.

The aloofness of Rome from the Ecumenical Movement fills so much of the picture that it is easy to overlook the fact that there are other churches also which do not participate in it. Contact with the Orthodox and Protestant churches which live behind the Iron and Bamboo curtains is difficult but none the less important. Within the Western world itself, however, there are bodies on the left wing of Protestantism which keep themselves apart. Some, like the Southern Baptists, do so because they distrust organizations anyway and particularly distrust a body like the World Council, which is international and interconfessional. Others do so because they hold eccentric beliefs and are so self-enclosed that it is difficult for them to have any kind of dealings with outside bodies. The Latter-Day Saints are such a group.

Others are Holiness Movements which, as yet, have too inchoate an organization and too limited a vision to be able to meet with other bodies on terms of equality. These groups are more numerous than might at first appear, and they deserve more sympathetic consideration from the well-established churches than they have yet received. There is a great deal of snobbery in the ecclesiastical realm, which is the more insidious because it is able to masquerade as theological or liturgical or disciplinary integrity. These groups are often one of the chief growing points of the Christian community as far as conversions from the world outside are concerned, and their chief strength lies among the quiet in the land, the poor and the humble. They have their grave weaknesses and vary greatly from each other in their Christian quality, but many of their weaknesses are the products of immaturity and ignorance rather than of ill-will. To find a place for most of them in the organization of the Ecumenical Movement may be difficult, and many of them will be very suspicious of it, but more mature and well-established churches should feel a stronger obligation than they generally do to try to enter into friendship with them. To do this may require tact and patience, but the enterprise is worth while both because these churches need help in ridding themselves of eccentric and misleading notions and in reaching a more spacious and generous understanding of the Gospel and because they themselves contribute much-needed vitality and freshness to the whole Christian community.

Churches in general need to remember that, in Western lands at least, they depend upon each other and need each other far more than they have been accustomed to admit. Thus the Roman Catholic Church in Britain and America draws most of its intellectual leadership from the ranks of dissatisfied Protestants and Episcopalians. Episcopalianism feeds on popular Protestantism, both for ministry and membership. Congregationalism draws much of its support from the ranks of those brought up in Fundamentalist or extremely conservative churches. The more conservative Protestant churches recruit new members from the Pentecostal sects. Churches need each other and should learn a new humility and sense of mutual care in their dealings with each other. The Pauline injunction about the way in which members of the body depend upon each other applies as much to the relations of denominations with each other as it does to the relations of individual members in particular churches. The standard of Christian conduct among denominations in dealing with each other, whether they are in a position to contemplate immediate reunion or not, is indefensibly low and must be reformed. All churches have much to repent of, all have much to learn from each other. All are called today to recover their vision of one Church in the one purpose of God, and to do so not as an optional extra for a few but as the way of obedience for all. To the extent to which they obey, they will also find that it is the way of renewal.

CHAPTER XVI

Extra Ecclesiam Nulla Salus

That there is no salvation outside the Church is a notion which most people, including members of churches, would be most reluctant to accept. Even Roman Catholics, for whom the belief has dogmatic authority and who leave their followers in no doubt as to what constitutes the true Church, frequently strain themselves very hard to find an interpretation of it which takes away its most obvious offensiveness and difficulty. Most Protestants rarely mention it these days, and some go out of their way to repudiate it.

There are, as we shall see, excellent reasons for this uneasiness. But it is always a good rule, when confronted by an apparently harsh and unreasonable doctrine to ask what it really says and why it ever appeared in the first place. The point of this doctrine is that it is the negative form of a positive insight. It arose in the first place because men really did find salvation inside the Church. Their experience of the presence of Christ was so vivid and the common life of the Church was so rich that they were clearly aware of a decisive difference between the Church and the world. Now, however, the lines between the Church and the world are very much more blurred. It is true that this may be partly because in many places the Church has successfully infiltrated the world with its own spirit, but it may be equally due to the fact that the world has successfully infiltrated the Church. We are perhaps too ready to suppose in these days that this question no longer presses upon us as acutely as it did on former generations because of our greater humility and liberality of temper. It may be due only to the Church's failure to apprehend clearly the reality of its salvation. To the extent to which it does so, this question again becomes living and urgent.

It has been one of the main themes of this book to insist that the Church is integral to the Gospel. It is the expression, in terms of this life, of the new relationship which men enjoy with God and with each other through what Christ has done for them. Whatever be our view of the institutional form which this expression should take, clearly it should have some form in terms of the dealings men have with God and with each other if their experience of God in Christ is to attest itself as genuine at all. Can there be any salvation outside some form of the Church, when the meaning of salvation is the recovery of that right relation to God and neighbors of which the Church is the concrete expression?

The question, therefore, is a serious one, and to fail to see it as such is to disqualify oneself from giving a responsible answer to it. At the same time, it is a question which admits of no simple answer. To answer it with overconfidence and possible arrogance, as many Christians have in the past and as some do today, is to be false to the character of the salvation which is to be found within the Church. There are several reasons which should prompt Christians to approach this question with particular humility and reserve in the present situation.

One reason is our greatly increased knowledge, which helps

us to see more clearly the relativity of many aspects of human religion and culture and their institutional manifestations. This may make us all the more convinced of the essential uniqueness and absolute validity of the Christian revelation of God, but it does so by making clear how fundamental are the levels of experience which that revelation addresses. This, in its turn makes us see how much its secondary manifestations and accompaniments and results partake of the relativity of all religion and culture. Many beliefs and procedures which most of our Christian forefathers believed to be essential to the continued existence of true Christian faith are now seen to be the fruit as much of their own particular situation as of the Gospel itself. This does not necessarily mean that they should be repudiated, but it does mean that the value we attach to them must be revised and that we have to consider again whether those who do not share them should be unchurched.

Another closely related reason is that it is now clear that the darkness in which those dwell who do not know and acknowledge Christ is not a simple and unrelieved darkness. It may be no less the duty of Christians than it ever was to convert the heathen, but what this conversion should involve is not self-evident nor is it clear that it should take the same form in every instance. What is self-evident is that the experience of the Church since the coming of Christ shows that Christians must beware of the dangers of seeking uncritically to make over those outside their company into their own image of the Christian life, because that image is excessively influenced by their own limited national or sectarian preconceptions. This is certainly no less true of those churches which self-consciously claim the title Catholic than it is of any other Christian bodies. The reasons for the resistance of large groups of people to the Christian faith in parts of the world such as the Islamic countries are not easy to fathom, but one of them is almost certainly that they dislike the dress in which Western Christians present it to them. Quite apart from this, there is the complicated matter of the relation in which other religious faiths, pursued with a devotion which often exceeds that shown by many Christians, stand to the Christian way of salvation. This is not the place to go into its complexities, which are full of pitfalls for the amateur and where superficial generalizations quickly mislead, but the very fact that the matter is so complicated prompts to further humility.

It may be very hard to see how salvation can exist outside the Church. It is no less hard to define with confidence the spiritual status of those who are outside. The maintenance of a proper Christian reserve is essential here. Christ tells His people to preach the Gospel to every creature. In order to do this, they must enter into the experience of those they address as sympathetically as possible. He demands that they give full value to that experience and neither take an unduly negative view of it, as the orthodox are disposed to do, nor an unduly positive one, as the liberal are disposed to do. But any conclusion they reach about the relation to Christ and His Church of those who are outside must come after and not before such a valuation.

Another important reason for hesitancy and humility in approaching this matter is that provided by the obviously ambiguous position of the churches in the world today. The difficulty of finding a universally acceptable definition of what constitutes the Church has already occupied our attention. The one thing which is surely clear to anyone but the most self-centered of denominationalists is that the Church cannot be identified without qualification with the churches. Not only are the churches divided, so that they compete with each other for the title of the ark of salvation, but their history over the last two thousand years has partaken of so much of the mutability of

human affairs and the limits of their visible form have been so
obviously conditioned by secular factors that any attempt at
rigidity quickly breaks down. What constitutes membership of
the Church? Are baptized members of a national church who
never attend, and who neither testify to spiritual experience nor
bring forth the fruits of holiness in their lives, members incor-
porate of Christ? And are faithful adherents of Baptist churches
with rigid standards of admission, who have not reached the
point of open profession and of baptism, outside the body of
Christ? To anyone who tries to keep close to spiritual realities,
the matter is clearly full of difficulties and uncertainties.

Of course it has always been obvious that many who show
little signs of bringing forth the fruits of the Spirit contrive to
enter the Church and become members in good standing.
Those who have insisted most strongly that outside the Church
there is no salvation have generally insisted no less strenuously
that membership of the visible body of the Church provides no
guarantee of salvation. Nevertheless, many people suspect that
to make the point that outside the Church there is no salvation
is to encourage those who are within to assume complacently
that they are the saved, in a self-righteous way which clearly
denies the Spirit of Christ. And, even if it be admitted that their
virtues are exaggerated by those interested in doing so, it is so
clear that many who are outside the Church do bring forth
fruits which are clearly those of the Spirit of Christ that the
question arises whether any content can be given at all to this
notion that outside the Church there is no salvation and
whether it is not better to drop the whole idea.

A further consideration arises here, which at the very least
supports the contention that this is an idea to handle with great
reserve in these days. It is that not only are modern churches
extremely ambiguous institutions, but the attitude of many people who do not share their life with them is extremely hard to

discover. The number of people, at least in lands like America and Britain, who have made a conscious act of rejection of Christ is very small. The vast majority of members of the community in these lands have been baptized, even though the number who have done much directly to implement their baptism is much smaller. Some of these people lead lives which are either openly immoral or else represent the kind of indifference which amounts to overt defiance of the will of Christ. It is hard to see how they can be held to be in any position other than that of sinful disobedience.

But most of them are not like that. They are people who are only too much like those who are active church members, with very similar virtues and vices. In some instances a case could be made out that they had taken the more Christian course in leaving the Church than they would have if they had remained in it. It is, unfortunately, true that Christ Himself would be expelled from some institutions which bear the name of churches, although they are not perhaps quite as numerous as critics of the churches allege. Those who have taken this course may belong to that latent church of which Paul Tillich speaks, which is composed of those who have caught a vision of the true end of mankind in Christ and who seek to express it in their personal dealings and in their zeal for social righteousness, but who are not gathered into church order with their brethren, either because they cannot see Christ in the churches they know or because they do not know that the vision they possess is that of Christ and of His people. It should be hastily added, however, that those who truly possess such a vision will not make invidious distinctions between themselves and the churches they know, nor will they congratulate themselves because they do not belong to them, but will realize their own frustration and loneliness and will anxiously inquire whether it is their own pride and not the sin of their neighbors which is preventing them from gathering into church order with them. In communities where churchgoing is unfashionable there are probably more Pharisees outside the churches than within them.

While that needs to be remembered, it remains true that the most fitting attitude on the part of members of churches toward most of their fellows in Western society is one which emphasizes their solidarity with them rather than their distinction from them. In a short story called "The Young Soldier," published in the *New Yorker* for April 2, 1954, Miss Sylvia Townsend-Warner describes her experience at her confirmation at the age of sixteen in St. Paul's Cathedral, London. A mild disturbance was caused during the service by the sudden and embarrassed exit of one of the confirmation candidates, a young sailor. At tea afterward her family discussed the possible reasons which might have prompted the sailor to leave so hurriedly. She confessed, however, that she had a deep conviction that his reason was that he had seen the unreality of the whole business and had had the courage to refuse to go on with it. And she went on to add that his action had prompted her to make the resolve that, as soon as she was free to do so, she would repudiate her own confirmation.

What is striking about the story, however, is the uncertainty in which we are left about the real meaning of the actions of the people involved. Miss Townsend-Warner did not know what the sailor's real motives were in leaving as he did. They may have been purely fortuitous or the exact opposite of what she imagined. Nor is it made clear what Miss Townsend-Warner was repudiating. Was it conventional Anglicanism and the solemn pretenses associated with mass confirmation at an early age, or was it the Christian faith itself? We are not told. This attitude is typical of many people outside the churches in our time. The Christian way of dealing with them is surely to regard them as fellow-members of the family of God, whose very reserve about the churches as they exist is to be taken as an occasion for self-examination on the part of those who are within the churches.

In the modern world, and especially on the more self-conscious levels of Western culture, we are members one of another to a far greater extent than most people realize. The difficulties about Christian belief and practice which are expressed by those outside the churches find their echoes in the minds of those within. The genuine affirmation and hopes of those within the churches find an inevitable response in the hearts of those without. We share a common way of life and a common destiny, and there are innumerable semiconscious and unconscious connections between our minds and hearts. Church members do well not to take too much at their own valuation what those outside say against their faith or to write them off as lost too readily. If God is able to work the miracle of faith in their own hearts, they have no right to suppose that He is unable to do the same in the hearts of people who are so similar to themselves. It is more true in modern Western society than it has been in most societies that those within the churches cannot be made complete themselves without the faith of those who are outside. The attitude of church members toward many of their fellows should, therefore, be more like that of St. Paul toward his fellow Jews than like that of the Jews to Gentiles.

These considerations need to be freely acknowledged and clearly borne in mind. A dogmatic temper on the wrong levels is a constant temptation in church life, and even today there are many members of churches who succumb to it. Yet, when all the necessary explanations and qualifications have been made, the fact remains that salvation means entering into a right relationship with God and with one's neighbor in His Spirit and being maintained in that relationship through the appointed means of His grace. It is also no less the fact that it is hard to see how

anyone who knows what this salvation means and who has the
opportunity to do so can refrain from joining in church order
with his fellow-Christian neighbors, if he wishes to continue in
saving fellowship with Christ Himself.

Furthermore, it can be claimed that, although the precise relation of a particular individual to the Church as it affects his
salvation is often so hard to determine that it would be inappropriate to try, experience proves that societies cannot continue long in health where the Church is persistently neglected.
There is a great deal of superficial thinking on this point,
especially on the part of those who imagine themselves to be
particularly emancipated and enlightened. It is true that when
the Church becomes timid, repressive, and conventional, as it
sometimes has in the bourgeois society of the West, breaking
away from it has seemed to work, not the promised death, but
only a more interesting form of life. But that only proves the
decadence of the church tradition. If those who break away do
not discover a richer or deeper form of church life, it is not very
long before the satisfactions which the world provides and their
own inherent vitality begin to lose their power. People become
bored and frustrated and find themselves more and more at
the mercy of wayward fashions and impulses. They lose, in fact,
the marks of that true manhood which the fourth chapter of
Ephesians described as the fruit of living in true church order
and become, as it says, "children tossed to and fro, and carried
about by every wind of false teaching, by the slight of men, and
cunning craftiness, whereby they lie in wait to deceive."

This process does not take place rapidly. In many instances it
takes more than one generation for it to happen, and it is more
visible in the history of a family than in the history of a particular individual. But today we can see very clearly how the
process has operated in many instances. A family is given discipline, integrity, and sometimes, though not invariably, prosper-

ity, as the fruit of the faith of one person or of a man and his wife. The children react against the piety of their upbringing, which may in part have been oppressive. Their lives still have some shape and meaning, however, because of their upbringing. They do not bring up their children in the way in which they were brought up. The children, for instance, are not trained to go to church, as they were when they were children. Their children must choose for themselves what they wish to do about religion, and meanwhile they will set them the unconscious example of treating it as of little importance in their own lives. The children have no standards and no clear direction for their lives. They become superficial hedonists and, unless some new factor enters into the situation, their lives become increasingly insignificant. Sin has, in fact, worked something which looks very much like death.

If observation of their behavior, especially as described in the novels they themselves praise, is any guide, the more fashionable parts of the great cities and resorts of the modern world are full of people of this type. The damage they do to their own lives and to that of society in general would be much more obvious if, in other parts of society, there were not many people who lived by other standards. It has been said that the history of many families is that the first generation is religious, the second learned, and the third worldly, and that the fourth has no history. That, of course, is a sweeping generalization, but the modern world provides enough illustrations of its truth to suggest that it is, at least, hard to find salvation very far away from the Church.

It will be clear from the whole argument of this section that the last thing any such reflections should do is to prompt any complacency among members of churches. The possibility of falling away from true obedience is open to all men, and churches themselves can turn into conspiracies against God.

Many of the people who have just been described have been misled because the marks of salvation were not clearly visible in the churches they knew. The most effective way in which those who are within can demonstrate to those without that salvation is to be found in the Church is by themselves living as humble, obedient, and joyful servants of Jesus Christ.

CHAPTER XVII

The Future of the Church

It is essential that this question should be looked at in the proper setting. Nothing is easier or more natural than to consider it on the purely journalistic level, in terms of those trends, whether hopeful or discouraging, which are visible in the various church situations of the world today. Those trends are, of course, of great and immediate importance in trying to answer this question, but they are far from being the only evidence which has to be taken into account, nor can they themselves be evaluated aright unless they are looked at in a wider setting.

Unless the Christian faith as a whole is founded on an illusion, it must be believed that the future of the Church is in God's hands rather than in those of men, and God's Spirit bloweth where it listeth. History is full of examples of the outbreak of its power in unexpected places and of its ability to confound all human expectations. The first sign of wisdom in this matter is to be cautious in prophecy, to beware of writing off as hopeless from the point of view of God's purpose places where the Church appears to have suffered defeat, and to avoid overcon-

fidence about situations where all seems to be well. It must also
be borne in mind always that, as we insisted at the beginning,
the future of the Church must be considered in the light of its
whole past, which is much longer than that period covered by
the memory of those now living. The proper question is not
simply what is likely to happen to the various denominations in
different parts of the world, but what is happening to that
stream of common experience which began with Abraham and
Christ and which has moved down throughout the ages to our
own day. Is it showing signs of disappearance or is it becoming
stronger and deeper?

The Christian way of looking at this matter should be sharply
distinguished from other ways. Perhaps it needs to be made
clear, however, that the Christian way is not necessarily in every instance the most optimistic. On the contrary, it is the way
which encourages men to look at history in the light of God's
revealed purpose for mankind, and that purpose says as much
about the sins and failures of churches as it does of individuals
and about the judgment which comes upon them. We have
seen that it is not difficult for churches to turn into conspiracies
against God, and that the Church against which the gates of
Hell shall not prevail cannot be identified without ambiguity
with those institutions which bear the name of churches. What
is more, the New Testament gives abundant warning that
churches may need the discipline of adversity to test their faith.
To know Christ is to share in the fellowship of His sufferings as
well as in the power of His resurrection. The fact that a church
may experience hard times does not necessarily mean that it is
in decline or that its faith in God has proved illusory. History
has shown again and again that God gives special blessings to
churches in such periods. Christians do not believe that the
forces of good constantly expand and grow stronger while those
of evil diminish. They believe that the good and the evil ripen

together unto the Day of Judgment. When the Church meets hardship or persecution instead of peace and prosperity, it does not follow that it is failing. Everything depends on the character of its reaction to these, but it could mean that the power of the good is so strong in the life of the Church that it is drawing out the power of evil in opposition to it. Any generalizations which are made about the future of the churches must, therefore, be qualified by our recognition of considerations such as these.

These considerations, however, reinforce the strength of the first point which must be made. That is that even the state of the present institutional manifestations of the Church in most situations indicates that it is not in process of fading away from the human scene. Indeed, that may seem so obvious to many today as not to need saying, but that is not so. For it had become a dogma of the various forms of secularism which flourished in the early part of the twentieth century that the churches were in decay, that their beliefs were discredited, and that their hopes for the future were illusory. Twenty-five years ago it was taken for granted in most self-consciously intellectual circles that for anyone to acknowledge himself a churchman was to confess his small-town simplicity and his ignorance of the ways of the great world. Had no one told him the facts of life? God, the God of the Church anyway, was dead. Clergy were fools or knaves, and their churches were places where hypocrites nursed their sense of moral superiority or the timid found a warm haven from the harsh blasts of reality. It was this conviction which between the wars attracted many serious-minded people either to Communism or to the various forms of scientific humanism which are still widely current. They believed that a new man had been born, emancipated, disillusioned, modern man, who had to make what he could of life with whatever resources his own courage and ability could muster up for him.

Now this modern reaction against the Christian faith among serious-minded persons has had many sides, and their relation to the Church is, as we saw in the last chapter, often extremely complex. Their attitude to the life of churches had a great deal of justification in many cases. There are churches whose God is dead and who survive by offering a form of religious escapism to those who find life too much for them. It is hard to believe that such churches have any positive future in the setting of God's eternal purpose, however much superficial success they may achieve. Little comfort need be derived from the recrudescence of religion of this type in our own time, the religion of "peace of mind" and of emotional individualism which avoids or oversimplifies life's problems. Yet the most stringent criticism of such religion comes from within the Christian faith itself, and our own time has witnessed a persistent prophetic vitality and many genuine signs of renewal in churches in many lands. So, far from dying, the churches are discovering once more the secret of being born again. The fact that this is so must present modern secularists with an acute problem. If what they have been saying for at least a generation is true, the churches have no right to continue and to grow in vitality and numbers. So far, most secularists evade the problem by denying or ignoring the existence of this revival of the churches.[1] The pages of papers like the British *New Statesman* are full of such denials or evasions.

Now this point is made not to rejoice over the discomfiture of those outside the churches but to encourage those who are within. As we also saw in the last chapter, there is much more affinity between what goes on in the minds and hearts of people in Western society than ever appears in their public statements, and members of churches have unquestionably been affected

[1]Some of the contributors to the famous *Partisan Review* symposium on "Religion and the Intellectuals" are among the few exceptions.

themselves by those doubts and uncertainties concerning the future of the cause to which they have committed themselves which have received open expression only in the public attitude of their opponents. The fact that many recent events have shown these doubts to be unfounded will help to release new energies within those who belong to the churches and confirm them in the hope that many of their contemporaries who remain outside will soon return.

It need hardly be emphasized that these events are not merely those connected with the rapid institutional expansion of the churches in some situations. That has its own importance, which should not be underestimated by superior persons. The instinct of the unreflective ordinary man, who goes with the crowd and who joins the Church for reasons which often appear superficial or conventional, may be shrewder than that of the intellectual, who is frequently unduly preoccupied with his own individual difficulties, in discerning which way history is moving. Besides, a mass movement toward the churches, such as is clearly visible in modern America, creates spiritual opportunities as well as dangers.

Yet the most significant and hopeful feature of the present Christian revival is not the numbers it affects but the quality of the experience which it engenders. One of the planks in the platform of most opponents of Christian faith was that the entity they described as "modern thought" had disproved it conclusively and that it could no longer exercise any compelling power over the mind of an educated person, except by a psychological trick whose influence vanished once its nature was exposed. This kind of attack can no longer be sustained in the face of the incontrovertible fact that Christian faith is able to give a more adequate interpretation of the nature of the human situation and to call upon stronger resources to act effectively within it than any of its modern rivals. This is not to say, of course, that it does not present serious difficulties to the human mind, but they are not, basically, different from those which it has presented from the beginning, and it has always vindicated itself as true not by evading them but by overcoming them in the practical experience of the life of faith. Certainly its survival power is proving much stronger against the pressures of the modern world than that of most of its secular rivals. It has been observed that it is extremely hard for an idol to survive for long in the modern world, as the brevity of the hold of Communism on the allegiance of most reflective intellectuals proves. "Is there a God beside me? Yea, I know not any," second Isaiah says, and it is not difficult for anyone looking out upon the world today to echo his words. If Christ is not the hope of the world, it is very hard to say who or what else can be.

Secondly, it appears that it can be confidently predicted that the future will not sustain the claims made by some religious bodies to be alone and exclusively the one true Church of Jesus Christ. Whatever the Church of the future may be, it will not be the Roman Catholic Church in its present form, nor will it be an amalgamation of churches possessing the "historic episcopate," nor will it be an exclusive fellowship of fundamentalist Protestants. Now this again may seem so obvious to many as hardly to require statement, but that is not so. After all, very large sections of Christendom are occupied by people who, to the extent to which they take their own positions seriously, would have to unchurch vast numbers of people who acknowledge Jesus Christ as Lord and who would have to insist that the only church with any positive future in the purpose of God is the church which they already are.

The most substantial and impressive claim along these lines is made, of course, by the Roman Catholic Church. It is pertinent to inquire, therefore, whether there are signs that, as history goes forward under the Christian dispensation, the truth of the

Roman claim is becoming more manifest and harder to resist for those who think in Christian terms. It is a question which is hard for a non-Roman Christian to answer without prejudice, but it is surely equally hard for a Roman Christian who tries to be without prejudice to explain away the massive amount of evidence which indicates that the Roman claim breaks down because it fails to cover all the hard facts of Christian experience. Churches come into being, prosper, reform themselves, and bring forth the fruits of the Spirit outside the Roman allegiance and independently of Roman influence, and they are showing more and not less ability to do so as time goes on. Rome makes some advances here and there, but when she does so it is often through a display of exceptional evangelistic zeal or tactical shrewdness. When she wins successes through the constraint of the manifest truth of what she says, it can frequently be shown that she is emphasizing something which is common to all Christian traditions rather than peculiar to herself. It is by preaching the atoning work of Christ for sin rather than the efficacy of the intercession of Mary, and by proclaiming the lordship of Christ in His Church rather than the authority of the see of Rome, that she wins her greatest victories. And while she may make advances here and there, they are not greater than those of Protestantism. Indeed, the effectiveness of Roman propaganda conceals the extent to which Rome has suffered major strategic defeats, not merely since the Reformation but also in the present century. She has lost far more souls to Communism than Protestant churches have, and done so in places more vital for her continuing life. Although she has been very active in the New World, the leadership and the characteristic institutions of the most vigorous and progressive parts of the New World remain firmly in hands other than hers.

The faithful member of the Roman Catholic Church will, of course, reply to this that temporary setbacks do not affect her ultimate triumph, since she has the promise of her Lord. It can, however, be pointed out to Rome that her Lord may be compelling her to reconsider her interpretation of that promise through making her see that her only hope of continuing in strength is by adjusting herself to the fact that He is able to work at least as effectively through Christians who repudiate the Roman allegiance as through those who acknowledge it. Necessity compels her to do this in many situations, even to the point of contradicting her official position. In every country where her members are not in an overwhelming majority she behaves in practice over many matters like one of the Christian denominations, and the attitude of many of her members toward her, whatever may be true of her priesthood, is not unlike that of members of other churches toward their own denomination. And we have seen that the rise of the Ecumenical Movement, in particular, presents Rome with the greatest challenge to her exclusive claim which has arisen since the Reformation.

It is to be hoped that, in time, Rome will respond positively to this challenge. Whether she does so or not, all the signs point to the fact that the Church of the future will not be purely Roman.

What is true of Rome is no less true of other churches which make exclusive claims. The interaction between Eastern Orthodox and the churches of the West will continue to produce results which are fruitful to both, but it is wildly improbable that in the measurable future the churches of the West are going to become Orthodox on Eastern terms. Whether Protestant churches are prepared to accept the "historic episcopate" by which many Anglicans lay so much store is a more open question, but it is clear that they will not accept it in any form which appears to imply that without it they have lacked something which is essential to their existence as churches. Again those Protestant sects who are so conscious of their own distinctive purity as to refuse to hold communion with other Christian bodies do not behave as though they seriously believe that their claim will be universally accepted among Christians, and the discernible trend of history certainly gives them no ground for encouragement.

This is closely related to our third point. The Christian way of thinking about the future, as we have seen, is to think about it prophetically. It is not so much to assess trends in ecclesiastical affairs as to interpret those trends in the light of God's declared purpose for all His people. It is, therefore, widely held among Christian people today that the chief special task to which God is calling His Church in the immediate future is that of the recovery of her broken unity in the pursuit of a renewed vision of the wholeness of the people of God in the setting of the whole world. This unity should have its institutional expressions, because it is in its institutional forms that the spirit of disunity is most deep-rooted and intractable. But whether the measure of institutional unity achieved by the various churches be small or great, they should all have a unity of spirit and of common work, as members of one family with a common mission as God's ministers of reconciliation to all mankind.

The central importance of this to the Church's future existence has already been emphasized in the chapter on the unity of the Church. It is questionable, however, whether the great majority of members of the Church realize how great the urgency of this matter is. The Christian view of history is that it is a field in which the good and the evil grow together unto the Day of Judgment. Evil has been growing to a very considerable degree of ripeness in our own day. There is, if we may put it thus, an ecumenism of evil in the modern world. Its nature is such that the poison of evil quickly spreads over wide areas of mankind, most spectacularly in matters of politics, but also in other spheres of personal relations. This ecumenism of evil can

be subdued and cast out only if the good grows and spreads
itself even more rapidly and effectively. The churches in every
land must give a new concreteness to their claim to live as one
family of God, whose unity transcends all barriers of nation and
race and class and denomination.

What this means in detail has been considered from time to
time in the course of our discussion, and it is the constant theme
of the many admirable reports which are brought out and commended to the churches by the conferences and assemblies of
the World Council of Churches. The danger is that many
churches will be content to take the publication of these reports
as a substitute for trying to implement their recommendations.
No church leaders can complain that they lack guidance for the
future in regard to the line of Christian duty, in regard to unity
and evangelism and missions and race relations and the function of the laity and the life of society. What they sometimes
lack is the sense of urgency which will prompt them to press
home their convictions with sufficient zeal and determination,
so that they effectively influence the life and action of their own
churches. Ministers sometimes shrink from confronting their
people with the full splendor of the ecumenical vision because
they fear that they will resist the changes of outlook and mode
of life which it will demand. This is a mistaken attitude. To be
warned persistently in sermons that there is no alternative between Christ and chaos, and then to be left with no significant
means of expressing obedience to Christ in forms relevant to the
needs of the time, is a much more frustrating and dishearten-
ing experience for people than to be confronted with specific
challenges to follow Christ and overcome chaos in this direction or that.

Besides, for churches to refuse these challenges is to succumb
to chaos, even though it may be concealed behind a façade of
well-equipped buildings and seemly rituals and properly certi-

fied ministries. Judgment begins at the house of God, and the possibility of being cast away is as real for particular churches as it is for individuals. The way to salvation is also the same for both. They must be prepared to die that they might live. And dying for churches means being prepared to surrender loyalties and associations which seem to them to make up the very substance of their life in order to venture forward into the unknown with the single assurance that Christ is leading them.

It is sometimes easy, though not invariably so, for churches to learn this lesson in hardship or persecution. Many churches in the world today are being given that opportunity. As far as the immediate future is discernible, however, that discipline is not likely to be imposed on many other churches, notably those of the English-speaking lands, and they have no right to tempt God by waiting for it. They have the duty of showing their readiness to die that they might live in a time when their existing institutions flourish and men speak comparatively well of them. That is not easy, but it is no less essential than showing faithfulness in persecution. Much is required of those to whom much is given. If the churches of America and Britain and of lands similarly placed do not rise to the height of their ecumenical opportunity in this century, we may be sure that it will go hard with them in the next.

CHAPTER XVIII

The Church and the End

The frequent painful changes and readjustments which are necessary to the continuing vitality of the people of God will be achieved with the necessary speed and resilience only if the Church keeps clearly before itself the fact that its final home is not to be found in this world but in that which is to come. God's people are "strangers and pilgrims on the earth," desiring "a better country, that is a heavenly." It is only as they press forward to their eternal habitation that God acknowledges them as His own, because "He has prepared for them a city" (Hebrews 11:16).

Protestant church life, in particular, has suffered a great deal because it has not shown much awareness of this dimension of its existence in recent generations. It has not thought much of the life to come, and when it has done so, it has often been chiefly in terms of the relation toward it of the individual and his own family and friends. That the reality of the day-to-day life of the Church should be determined by its relation to that which is to come has not been obvious to most of modern Protestantism. It has believed that the Church should make progress, certainly, but it has thought of it chiefly as a progress toward its own institutional prosperity and toward general social betterment rather than toward its final end in Christ.

This attitude has its good side. Part of its concentration on the immediate task in hand has been due to a healthy acceptance of the fact that God makes His will known only here and now and that, if we are faithful in the present situation, the future can safely be left in His hands. The habit of neglecting the obligations of this life in passive contemplation of the joys of another has never had the wide currency in churches that the Church's critics imagine. Only a minority of people are able to achieve that measure of otherworldliness, even of a false kind. But a vague desire for comfort and reassurance about one's condition both in this world and the next, for what is now often called "peace of mind," without being unduly troubled by the more venturesome and costly aspects of Christian duty, undoubtedly has had and still possesses a wide currency. Protestant activism has been a healthy protest against that, and its protest is not needed less today than in the past. It has also to be said that the Catholic emphasis on the reality of the other world, for which the rest of Christendom has had cause to be grateful in recent times, has not been free either from the excessive individualism which has marked some forms of modern Protestantism or from a certain unhealthy morbidity. There is an oppressive, anxious quality about Requiem Mass or about an otherwise rich and noble work of Catholic piety like the "Dream of Gerontius," both in Newman's poetry and in Elgar's music, which warns us that preoccupation with death and the life to come can be enervating as well as salutary.

Yet the dangers of this attitude are greater than its merits. For when the Church ceases to consider her life without reference to her ultimate end, she becomes secularized in the most precise and radical way. There are at least two reasons for this.

In the first place, churches cannot evade the issues raised by the challenge of death any more than individuals can. They must face it honestly and overcome it if their faith is to be surely grounded. This is true of all churches in all situations. In the preliminary discussions of the Christian Hope before the Evanston Assembly of the World Council of Churches, it was frequently suggested that the preoccupation of some members of the World Council with questions of eschatology, the study of the final realities of existence, was due to the experiences through which Europeans, in particular, had passed in the tragic events of the last few decades. It was further implied that the happier experience of America made it less necessary for Americans to occupy themselves with such matters. Fortunately this was by no means a universal attitude among Americans, because it is hard to think of a more superficial approach to the question. Is death an un-American activity? Surely the fundamentals of the human situation in the light of God's eternal purpose are not radically different from one place to another. All men are united in the need to come to terms with the greatest crisis of human experience and to know that God can sustain them through it if their faith in Him is to be real. When they try to pretend, in comfortable, well-upholstered societies, that they can ignore or evade it, they are living a lie. It is not the Bible which is escapist in regard to death, nor, for that matter, the traditional practice of the Church, as the sober realism of the burial service in the Book of Common Prayer indicates. It is the popular modern funeral-parlor sentimentality, which, by sparing no expense, contrives to soften the impact and challenge of death to such an extent that it hopes no one will notice that it has happened. Churches cannot survive for long in such an atmosphere.

The other reason is that indifference to final realities encourages people to look at the function of the Church in this present world in the wrong perspective and, in so doing, to be misled even in regard to immediate Christian action. The assertion that to pay attention to eschatology promotes a conservative indifference to matters of Christian duty here and now has no justification. It is true that people are always looking for excuses to do nothing, and that they can twist this, as they can everything else, to serve that purpose; but the New Testament experience of life which is life indeed in Christ, which is but a foretaste of the fullness of life in glory and which impels forward those who possess it to give it expression in the midst of "this present age which passeth away," has proved itself to be a most liberating and creative force in all history.

The reasons for this are clear to anyone who has some knowledge of that experience. Unless men know that they possess Christ as a permanent reality, no matter where they may be in space or time, and that they will continue to know Him only as they move forward with His Spirit to the fulfillment of all things in Him, which will not take place under the conditions of life as we know it on this earth, they are inevitably disposed to find the meaning of their existence in those things in the Church's life which are secondary and derivative. They forget that they are strangers and pilgrims. They settle down and make themselves at home in the temporary resting places which God provides for their refreshment on this earth. They carefully delimit the boundaries of these encampments. They make rules and regulations for their life as though the only situations which could arise where they might need guidance would be those which do so in the well-defined and calculable internal life of the camp. They incline more and more to be governed by precedent, to cherish the traditions of camp behavior and to give much attention to matters of rank and hierarchy. When anyone suggests that they strike camp and move forward, a host of reasons quickly present themselves which convince

them that this is not the moment for doing so. They have too
much baggage and it would raise too many problems for the
administration.

That this has happened to many churches in the course of
history is obvious. Catholic churches may have proved themselves the most efficient at organizing this process, but all
churches undergo it to some extent. There can be little doubt
that the reason why so many of them find it hard to undertake
any risky new venture or to reunite with other churches is that
they no longer trust in Christ but only in the life and organization of their own earthly encampments, in which they seek to
trap Him. But let the fact be forced upon their attention that
their home is not here but above, that the most imposing ecclesiastical structure is but a lodging in the wilderness and that the
means of grace they receive there are but refreshment to give
them new strength for the next stage of their journey to their
homeland, and they are released for action once more. They
become truly the Church *in via* again, and risks and bold experiments become part of their normal existence. They recover
living faith in Christ, and with His Spirit before them as a pillar
of cloud by day and of fire by night, they are prepared to venture forward into the unknown, confident that when they reach
their destination He will be there to meet them.

So far is this concern for the end from being an un-American
activity that Americans of all people should be the first to understand it and insist upon its importance. The people who
have been taken by most Americans as the chief founders and
archetypes of their national existence were known as the Pilgrim Fathers. They were pilgrims, not because they were
rugged adventurers who set forth with indomitable self-confi-
dence to find a place where they could enjoy "liberty of conscience," as some of their children who were out of sympathy
with their spirit have found it convenient to suppose, but be-

cause they believed that their venture was a necessary stage in their journey to the heavenly City. They knew that they were strangers and pilgrims on the earth, whose true security and hope lay in God and whose salvation lay in the fulfillment of His great design. The wild ocean and "the howling wilderness" on which they landed held no terrors for them because they knew that they were always able to "cast up their eyes to heaven, their only true country." They knew that God would be with them in New England as He had been in old England and in their exile in Holland, and that, though they were leaving home and friends and kindred and the established Church of their own land, He would provide heavenly food for His people. There may have been some elements of presumption in their attitude, and not all their expectations were fulfilled, but they believed that God had vindicated their faith and they would never have dared to take the risks which they did unless they were confident of His final triumph. The children of the Pilgrim Fathers, who sometimes appear content to settle not for their fathers' spiritual kingdom but only for the earthly kingdom which is the visible fruit of their faith, need to ask themselves whether they fully understand the terms on which spiritual adventure is alone possible. A spirit of enterprise and a free mind are not engendered simply by singing their praises. They come only as the fruit of the faith of people who live in this life as those who have been made the freemen of another.

It is clearly essential, therefore, that the Church, if it is to survive, must regain the perspective of the New Testament in its relation to the life to come. It is true that, as we have frequently emphasized, the foundation of the Church lay in an experience of the present reality of the promised Kingdom in the midst, through the indwelling Spirit of Christ. There is a sense in which eternity is present here and now, as the Fourth Gospel insists when it speaks of eternal life or its synonym life, which is life indeed. It is not always seen that the tremendous words of Hebrews, "Ye are come unto mount Zion, and unto the city of the living God, the heavenly Jerusalem, and to innumerable hosts of angels, to the general assembly and church of the first-born who are enrolled in heaven, and to God the Judge of all, and to the spirits of just men made perfect, and to Jesus the mediator of a new covenant" (Hebrews 12:22–24), are all in the present tense. This is the Good News which the Church proclaims, that in the midst of "this present age" which passes away, men can live by the powers of "the age to come" which overcome "this present age."

Yet it is obvious that, although the Church does possess this power, the evil powers of "this present age" remain active and need to be overcome. The Church still lives on earth and not in heaven. The nature of the experience of eternal life which she enjoys is such that it points men forward to seek its more complete fulfillment and to hasten the time when heaven and earth shall meet. Christ does speak in the Spirit to men here and now, as their contemporary, but what gives significance and urgency to that speaking is that His people must heed and obey Him so that they are in an appropriate position to welcome Him when He comes again. The words of the passage in Hebrews are in the present tense but they go on to say, "See that ye refuse not him that speaketh." He who speaks is the One who will come again with power to gather all things to Himself and to receive His own. Otherwise, His words lack ultimate authority.

When the Church cries, "Even so, Lord Jesus, come," her cry is not a prayer for escape offered by those who are weary of this life and long to be released from its agony. There are some Christians, languishing in the bondage of harsh captivity or racked with pain from which there is no respite, who are entitled to pray in that way. In its essence, however, this is a cry of fulfillment rather than of despair. It means, "Come,

Lord Jesus, manifest that righteousness we struggle imperfectly to achieve here below. Make up that which is lacking in our own halting obedience. Give permanence to that beauty of which we catch only fleeting and broken glimpses in this world. Fulfill that communion with Thyself and with each other for which we long and which we never establish." The proof of the sincerity with which that cry is uttered is the zeal with which the Church seeks to express that for which it prays in the present moment.

The time in which the Church sees itself as living is that which lies "between the times" of its reconciliation with God in Christ and its full redemption, when He gathers all things to Himself. That Christ reigns as King over mankind is not yet made manifest in such a way that all men see it, but it is the "mystery," in St. Paul's sense of "the open secret," which the Church celebrates and by which it lives in the midst of a world which passes away. All the forms of this world, and these include even the earthly forms of the Church, will pass away with it, and the Church does well not to treat them with final seriousness, but as long as it retains its contact with the eternal Spirit of Christ, it can be of good cheer. The Spirit is the earnest of its inheritance, and with its guidance the Church knows that it is able to pitch its traveler's tent each day "a day's march nearer home."

Once again let it be emphasized that these familiar expressions of traditional piety refer primarily to the Church rather than to the individual believer. This is the time of the Lord's patience, in which He permits evil to wax for a season, that He might test the faith of His people and give all men an opportunity to repent and believe. It is also the time of the Church's hope, for it knows that, whatever may happen on the surface of life, God's triumphant purpose moves inexorably forward and that He is preparing His people for their habitation which is from heaven.

It is this conviction of God's final triumph and of the participation of all whom Christ has claimed for Himself in that triumph which lies behind the Church's belief in the communion of saints. This is another aspect of the Christian faith which has dropped out of the consciousness of many modern Protestants but which is essential to an adequate understanding of the Church.

The saints in this instance are not, of course, only those departed Christians of outstanding holiness who have been canonized by some sections of the Church. They are the whole company of Christ's faithful people, including both those who have died in Christ and those who follow Him now on earth. They are, in fact, the Church in its most inclusive sense, militant on earth and triumphant in heaven. There are wide differences between churches about the way in which they think of this communion, but all are agreed that, as the Apostles' Creed declares, it is a reality and a greatly cherished one.[1]

At the same time, it cannot be denied that many Christians have great difficulties in grasping what is involved in the communion of saints. One reason for its comparative neglect in some Protestant churches in recent times has been that they have a more honest apprehension of those difficulties than have some churches which have continued to develop their teaching along the lines of their own tradition without constantly checking it by experience. After all, the primary emphasis of the New Testament in speaking of the communion of saints is on the communion which God's people enjoy with each other while they are on earth together. That may have been partly due to the fact that the New Testament was written at a time when only a

---

[1] See the *Report of the Conference on Faith and Order,* Edinburgh, 1937, Chapter IV on the Communion of Saints.

small proportion of the saints had "fallen asleep," but it was also due to its great reserve concerning the nature of the life after death. It is true that, especially in its later portions, the New Testament gives visions of what the life of the saints in glory will be like. But they are only visions; they are not precise statements of verifiable facts. Little more is said in general of the state of those who die in the Lord than that they fall asleep in Christ and rest in Him, and that at the last all who abide in Him shall have part in the general resurrection. Specific notions about an intermediate state or the intercession of the saints on our behalf or about messages sent by them to those on earth have little justification on biblical grounds.

Yet the simple fact that all God's people continue to live as one family in Him, even though some are divided from others by "the narrow stream of death," itself carries rich implications. It means that Christian people can say with confidence that the Christ who gives meaning and vitality to their own life on earth is available to those who have gone before them, and that they can enjoy life in Him without the corruption and distortion which inevitably accompanies it here below. They are at least one stage further than we are toward the fulfillment of Christ's purpose for them. Where they have gone, it is good for them to be. And because we also are with Christ, as they are, we hold communion with them through Him.

It is not easy to give specific content to this experience of communion, and the fact that, at this point, so much Christian teaching takes refuge in pious generalization is particularly unfortunate. There is only one clear point of reference in this matter, and that is indicated by the words "through Jesus Christ our Lord." Jesus Christ does not speak directly to us here and now, "as a man speaks with his friend." We know Him only through the Spirit, which makes His words come alive for us as words spoken to our condition. But that is real personal knowledge,

knowledge which affects our life on the same level as does that
of other people. Yet that knowledge is never knowledge of
Jesus Christ in isolation. His Spirit leads us into the realm
where He is King, and it is a fair and goodly place, "where the
shining ones dwell." When Jesus Christ comes to us in the Spirit,
He brings His saints with Him. What makes the Church possible is the reality of the communion which Christ's people hold
with Him and with each other in His Spirit. If that communion
is destroyed by death, "we are still in our sins and are of all
men the most miserable." As the living Christ holds communion
with the Church on earth, so He does with those who died in
the Lord. That means that, through Him, the Church on earth is
able to enter into the same universe of discourse as the Church
in glory. The concerns of the members of the Church in glory
for the Church in earth are incorporated into those of Christ as
He speaks to the Church on earth in the Spirit. Through Him,
therefore, they hold communion together. It is an indirect communion, and it is dangerous to suppose that it can be anything
else. Christian experience is full of examples of how individuals
and churches can be misled if they seek direct contact with
members of the Church in glory, whether canonized or not. The
fact that it is indirect does not, however, mean that it is unreal
or insignificant.

That the members of the earthly Church cannot see and
speak with those they loved and worked with who now live
with Christ is a serious deprivation, which gives point to the
longing which many older Christians have that God may
quickly call them to join those whom they love. Yet they have
the consolation that the communion they already enjoy with
them through Christ is purer, if less direct, than that which they
knew when they walked and talked with them. For what they
hold communion with is that which was of Christ in them,
which they only imperfectly realized on earth, but which is now

fulfilled. The witness of the saints which inspires the Church is not merely that of their earthly life but of that life glorified and fulfilled in the eternal purpose of God.

It is essential that the elaboration of ideas such as these for purpose of edification should be strictly controlled by what sure knowledge we have of the working of the Holy Spirit. When that is done, it can be claimed that they vindicate themselves in experience in the indirect way in which many other parts of Christian teaching do. They give men the most creative attitude possible toward the life of those who have gone before them, and they also give a hope for the future which transforms the crisis of death and provides meaning for life here and now. If it is true that here, more than in most places, we are conscious of dwelling in a realm of mystery, it is also true that the benefits which the communion of saints brings are real and effective. Those who are bereaved testify that the threat of meaninglessness which death carries is overcome, that strong consolation is given, and that the witness of the saints actively inspires those they leave behind with courage to go forward.

In these days, when men have tried to live without God and have found again that sin does indeed work death, the Church cannot speak to their condition unless it does so with all the resources of Christ. It cannot draw upon those resources unless it recovers its unity, and that unity is not merely the unity of the visible body of Christ but also the unity of the whole eternal family of God. We are strangers and pilgrims on the earth, but a great host whom no man can number follow every step of our journey and encourage us with their help. It is true that we keep closest to them by keeping close to Christ in His Spirit, but He would not have us unaware that they are with Him. It is because they are with Him that we may hope to be with Him also, and it is that hope which inspires our action in the present. A writer in *Time* magazine commented wryly of the Evanston

Assembly of the World Council of Churches that in the twentieth century, apparently, it is news that Christians believe that
there is hope for mankind. It is always news, for it is never
self-evident. It is the Church's task now, as always, to declare
that hope through living by it daily, in communion with the
eternal family of God in Christ.